WHAT THE MOUTH WANTS

Caitlin Press Inc.
8100 Alderwood Road, Halfmoon Bay, BC V0N 1Y1
www.caitlin-press.com

Text and cover design by Vici Johnstone
Cover and interior illustrations by Sheryl McDougald
Printed in Canada

Caitlin Press Inc. acknowledges financial support from the Government of Canada
and the Canada Council for the Arts, and the Province of British Columbia through
the British Columbia Arts Council and the Book Publisher's Tax Credit.

Library and Archives Canada Cataloguing in Publication
Meneghetti, Monica, 1967-, author
    What the mouth wants : a memoir of food, love and
belonging / Monica Meneghetti.

ISBN 978-1-987915-35-8 (softcover)

        1. Meneghetti, Monica, 1967-. 2. Meneghetti, Monica, 1967- –Family.
3. Bisexual women–Canada–Biography. 4. Catholics–Canada–Biography.
5. Italian Canadians–Biography. 6. Bisexual women–Identity. 7. Non-
monogamous relationships. 8. Autobiographies. I. Title.

HQ75.4.M46A3 2017   306.76'63092   C2016-907712-8

WHAT
THE MOUTH
WANTS

A Memoir of Food, Love and Belonging

Monica Meneghetti

Dagger Editions

Some of the names in this book have been changed to protect the privacy of the individuals.

For my mom, *l'ombra al mio fianco*.

Contents

ACKNOWLEDGEMENTS

"Late bloomers' stories are invariably love stories," wrote Malcolm Gladwell in the October 20, 2008, issue of the *New Yorker*. My story proves him right.

Sheldon, without your titanium brand of love and character, and your tireless dedication over the past twenty-one years, I would not have this life or this book. Thank you for teaching me to laugh about everything. Tasha, without your adventurousness, courage, patience and sweetness, I would not still be living this dream-come-true nine years later. Your passion for cooking inspired me, revived my love of food, and affirmed the meaning I place on an excellent meal. And thank you to my sister, who believed in my talent before I had anything to show for it, and who gave me *The Artist's Way* by Julia Cameron – a book that transformed my creative life.

My friends are amazingly supportive. Thanks are due especially to Jane Bateman for her sensitive, insightful reading of my early drafts and proofreading of the final ones; Rachel Iwaasa for her wise counsel and rare fusion of aesthetic insight and keen intellect, as well as proofreading; Mette Bach for laughing, listening and encouraging; and Tina McAlister for reminding me "finishing is good enough." Gratitude to my Treehouse Collective, Laurie Dawson and Kim Mayberry. We swung our feet over the void and boosted one another closer to our dreams. I was also fortunate to meet a pack of cuddle monsters who generously nurtured and energized me during the final months of writing the initial manuscript.

My writing is an expression of that vital energy which is known by many names: spanda, pneuma, shakti, spiritus, qi, mana, ruach, vril, ki … Inspired by Dylan Thomas' poem, I call it "green-fuse force." May it ever flow through me.

I am deeply grateful for my spiritual communities, especially my past and present guides on the path: Cindy Pujos-Michel, Carole Harmon, Anne Douglas, Lynn Swift and Gary Sill.

Numerous people have helped me to dig deeper and hone my craft, beginning with Jim Bedard, my grade ten English teacher, and culminating with UBC faculty members Wayne Grady, Susan Musgrave and Sioux Browning. Heartfelt thanks also to my mentors at The Banff Centre Writing Programs, Candas Jane Dorsey, Daphne Marlatt and Elizabeth Philips. Without all of you, I would never have come this far.

Jan Sommer and Glenn Watterberg, thank you for coaching me through the emotionally rigourous process of writing memoir. Thanks also to Eric Maisel whose book, *Fearless Creating*, has guided me through the various anxieties of the creative process for many years.

Bringing this project to fruition required a few final key ingredients: Fabian's intrepid heart, playful spirit and nurturing wisdom; Vici Johnstone's publishing acumen and the combined expertise of her Dagger Editions team; the insightful, frame-changing questions of Candace Elder (Creative Insight Coaching) and Melina (Radical Relationships Coaching); and the safety net of an extremely diverse and resilient community of queers and polyamorists in Cyberspace, Vancouver, and beyond.

Without the work of countless courageous writers, I would never have found the internal strength to be who I am, much less write it on a page: Robyn Ochs, Pepper Mint, Lani Ka'ahumanu and Loraine Hutchins, Dossie Easton and Janet Hardy, Carol Queen and Lawrence Schimel, Timothy J. Anderson and Candas Jane Dorsey, and Anaïs Nin, to name a few.

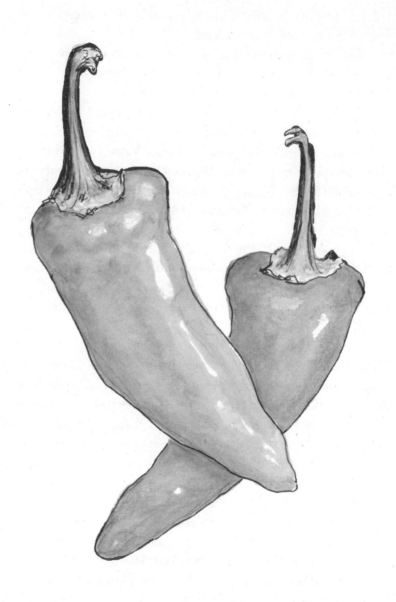

ANTIPASTI

Tongue

The tongue lies inside. Inside, right from the start. Inside our fetal mouths, jaws, heads. Inside the sac, inside the womb.

The tongue lies within. Within, from the beginning. Within the pelvis, within the flesh. Within nerves, skin, aura, air. Solar system, Milky Way and cosmos.

The tongue lies at the epicentre of life's vibrating ripple, in the pool of energy we call "alive."

The tongue knows nothing but fluid until, like the first nub of growth from an underground bulb, our thumbs extend to probe the orifice called mouth for the first time. Our first penetration is self-penetration with this soothing flange. And the thumb will be followed by air, by nipple, by milk, and from then on many things will enter our mouths, until our bodies cease to exist. Our survival depends on it.

And the tongue is witness to all of this insertion, be it intrusion or feast.

The tongue learns to shape vibrating exhalations into intelligible sound and invites the lips to co-create. The tongue wields words, oiled wood or acute steel words, keen stone or rough club words, until our bodies cease.

The tongue discovers other tongues. Beginning with the first tongue that thumbs its way between our lips, be they parted or clenched, the tongue recognizes itself in another and exclaims in pleasure or disgust. The tongue recognizes its own power in that other wetness.

The tongue rediscovers nipple, be it responsive nub or dumb kernel, remembers what we choose to forget: hunger assuaged with spray of milk; the latex-nipple cheat; the fulfillment, the safety, the drowse of mammalian communion.

The tongue may discover thumb's longer, unjointed cousin and its bitter milk of seeds. Or the one that never lengthened, instead hardened into another kind of nub that witnesses the tongue, greets it with tongue-like slickness but speaks an altogether different, pulsing language.

The tongue is supreme pontifex of flesh. A drawbridge lowered across the moat of the mouth. A bridge going both ways, connecting our minds with the ears of others and, hopefully, their hearts. A slick cobblestone bridge. The world trips or gallops over, creeps or charges into us. Rooted in the near shore of self, its link with the other shore is temporary, the passage easily withdrawn. Asleep, the tongue simmers in its own flavour. Awake, it savours the taste of inward-turning.

The tongue knows its buds will never flower yet responds ever-liquidly, remains ever-presently participant and witness.

BABY OCTOPUS

I have to imagine the scent of garlic and ocean tempting me into the kitchen. The bright flowers of my mother's cotton housedress, and olive oil pouring honey-yellow into a ceramic bowl. Mom's hands grasping the twin, black handles of the *mezza luna*, rocking its crescent blade across garlic and fragrant herbs. Her neatly manicured fingernails, smooth with clear polish. This must have happened.

Did I look over the rim of the bowl? If so, she must have taken it from the countertop and lowered it to my level, bending slightly at the waist. Her fingers would have splayed against the glaze as she held the bowl within range of my view. On the outside, glaze the green of pistachio *gelato*. On the inside, white as *latte*.

I am sketching in details. Tiny, fleshy creatures nestled against each other in the bowl. The reddish pink of their insensate tentacles. Suckers cupping minced parsley.

I deduce it was a blustery afternoon: my brother was at the school field, flying a kite.

"*Vai, diglielo la cena è pronta,*" she must have said, sending me to fetch him home for supper.

I would have run into the backyard, vaulted onto my bike and pounded the pedals up the back alley to the nearby field of the Protestant school.

But I do remember the joy. I remember sunshine and wind in my face, and flying toward my brother, and that long, thin cord of knowing which way was home. I remember singing "baby octopus, baby octopus!" all the way there.

THIRST

At the kitchen table, Mom pressed Dad's shirts on the brown
blanket from Bolivia, ancient white Inca designs padding polished
wood. Home from school, I'd find her tucking the small, curved
pillow into a cuff or shoulder, holding the spray bottle's lone arm,
misting from its red eye. I'd tell her of my day over the release of
steam and the gulping sounds coming from the iron, and lose myself
in the tiniest details.

   Until she said it. *Spremi l'arrancia!* Squeeze the orange, get
to the point. Said it until she didn't have to say it anymore, only
gesture with that squeeze-release, squeeze-release of her fist
around imaginary fruit. But there was no juice. Only my thirst for
her attention.

Halved Fruit

Mom's underwear hangs on the clothesline. Plastic-coated branches smoothed and ranked into unclimbable lines, rustling with white and beige. Looking up through the nylon foliage of high-waisted panties, I lose myself in fragrant brassieres hanging like halved fruit linked only by their skins. Reaching up, I pluck.

Convex fabric camouflages my flat chest. My eyes venture inside cantaloupe-sized cups. My nose, lips, cheeks and chin follow. My entire face fits within a single half.

Raw

The sprinkler thucks a steady rhythm like a big hand ticking its way around a clock. Then it reverses, rewinding time. A stream of water sparkles an arc across the lawn. The neighbour's Welsh corgies bark and chase a car's tires as it heads for the back of our cul-de-sac.

Joan and I sit on the rise at the boundary of my front yard. Green grass prickles the backs of my warm, bare thighs. I lick my index finger to the second joint. I stick it into a foil-lined packet, wiggle it around in purple powder, then put it back into my mouth. Sweet-and-sour, imitation grape flavour bursts against my tongue. I suck on my finger while drawing it out of my mouth. It pops out with the airy, puckered sound of *p*. A cork coming out of a bottle.

Joan also uncorks. We extend our tongues to each other for inspection. Stained. Like our fingers.

"I heard the big crystals in here cause cancer," I tell her.

She squints at the packet. "Maybe we should switch to Kool-Aid."

Then we lick-dip-suck and lick-dip-suck our sweet syncopation, keeping beat with the sprinkler until our tastebuds are raw.

ICE CUBE

My sister and I on summer vacation, hanging out in the half-base-ment family room. My toes scrunch and unscrunch against the couch's rough orange warp and white weft.

Instant iced tea and curtains shield us from the afternoon heat. Spock's eyebrow is arched while Kirk laughs at Bones' joke. Ba-dum-tschh of playful music, then credits roll.

I drink my last drop of iced tea and eye my sister's nearly emp-ty glass. She puts it on the coffee table next to mine. At the bottom of her glass floats a shiny, whiteish oval on a tiny pool of tea. Aha! One last ice cube, almost melted!

When her attention shifts to Richie Cunningham, I make my move.

The glass is warm in my hand. The warm cube creeps over my tongue and oozes down my throat.

"That was weird," I say.

"Ee-yewwww! You just drank my *gob*!"

NUTRITIONAL TORTURE

Before my tastebuds gauged the taste of tripe, I was living inside you, innocent of such Italian delicacies.

Before my nose knew aroma from stench; before I had teeth to gnaw the rubbery, gilled surface; before my throat could gag on the worm-like flesh; before I knew it was "cow's stomach" or even what "cow" or "stomach" meant, I had no need for pulling faces and you, no need to admonish me for it. *Non fare la smorfia*, you'd say while serving up those hideous strips stewed in tomato sauce.

Trippa. More reviled than liver or tongue, more dreaded than *baccalà* – that ram-rod salt cod standing on its tail in a water bucket near the washing machine, stinking for days as it softened.

Long before you locked me in the bathroom with *trippa* and shoved another plateful through the door when you heard the toilet flush, I was lounging in uterine brine, my face relaxed and smooth as a marinated mushroom, my guts naïvely willing to digest whatever you fed me.

Beyond the umbilical lies tripe. Had I known, I would have spelunked to your fallopians and bribed some other ovum forth to take my place. To save my face.

Green Peas

A white fence of painted wood surrounded our backyard. A passage-way ran between the fence and the right side of a detached garage. The passageway was a few feet wide. It led to a dead end and a big box built into the fence. We lifted the lid of the box to put garbage into two cans of galvanized steel.

From the top of that plywood lid coated in flaking white paint, I would look over the fence into the alley. It was the only place I could get a vista without leaving the safety of our yard. In my imag-ination, the garbage chute was a treehouse. I coveted other kids' playhouses and treehouses.

There wasn't much to see from my perch on the garbage-chute-slash-fort. The neighbours' own fences and open garages. A kid's bicycle carelessly dropped by one handlebar while the tires were still rolling, another propped on its kickstand, triangular orange flag fluttering atop a thin stick affixed to the frame. The occasional glimpse through kitchen sheers of pink latex gloves wielding sponge against dirty dish. Vegetable gardens with glossy black soil dividing ranks of obedient vegetables, others with lumpy grey soil disrupted by rampant weeds.

I always noticed the green peas, whether their tendrils slumped, or clambered and clung like dusty gymnasts to green dowels. My gaze sought out fat pods, remembering my mom's story.

In Italy, when my brother and sister were small, they came across a vendor selling peas in the pod and ran to Mom for some *lire*. They came home later with stomach cramps and diarrhea. It turned out they'd gotten their metric weights mixed up and asked for *due kili* instead of *due etti*, two kilos instead of two hundred grams – and they had eaten all two kilos between them.

The story amused me – my big sister and big brother making a mistake instead of me for a change! – yet it was strange to hear about things my siblings had done without me. At that point, my entire life had been lived within the context of my family. The story was evidence of the family having existed without me, before me. How peculiar and uncomfortable.

Perhaps my obsession with green peas was an attempt to reach back in time and insert myself into their history. I, too, wanted to eat a whole garbage bag full of fresh peas and get an upset stomach! In the suburbs, there were no vendors, only domestic gardens. So, I orchestrated a garden raid. In broad daylight, a couple of neighbourhood kids and I ran through all the backyard gardens, stripping peas and stuffing them into a black garbage bag. Disappointingly, we ran out of gardens before the bag was full.

We climbed onto my garbage chute/treehouse and started to eat, throwing empty pods over the fence into the middle of the alley. We were down to the last few pods when Mom came down the passageway to confront us. Someone had called her. Your daughter is a thief, the neighbour might have said. Pretending I was a pirate breasting the wind on the prow of a corsair, I tried to deny the accusations. But the verdant remains littering the alleyway were as incriminating as blood evidence. To make matters worse, my share of the booty hadn't been even remotely close to a stomach-churning two kilos.

NUT

My up-the-street neighbour's cheeks puffed out further than her boobs but she spoke with a brogue.

We were turning twelve. Back then, folks didn't lock their garages. Lawnmowers crouched undefended. Doors opened automatically and fake wood lay on walls and wagons.

The tool box in the back of the station wagon was a dirty, glossy red. The bolt we found smelled like the taste of a battery. She dared me to be the nut for this bolt, so I pressed it against my panties and felt metal and cotton threads meshing.

She gave me expert advice on how to get it in.

Her dad must have been a mechanic.

STEAK FAT

On our dinner plates, green peas nestle up against t-bone steaks of Alberta beef. My dad sits at the head of the table, my brother at his right hand and me at his left. My mom sits beside me, and my sister opposite her. The other end of the table butts up against the wall.

I'm listening to my teenaged brother talk about his day. My dad starts mocking him about something. My brother is obviously annoyed by this, but my dad doesn't let up.

My brother picks up a piece of steak fat from his plate.

"Say that again and I'll throw this at you."

Dad says it again.

"I'm serious," my brother says. "Once more and I'm throwing it."

Dad, once more. My brother flicks his wrist. Steak fat smacks against Dad's cheek and he roars upright, right hand flying out in an arc bound for his son's head.

Next thing I know, my brother's sitting stunned on the floor, surrounded by scattering green peas. Silence. His plate hula-hoops against linoleum. Before it can reach stasis, Dad is on his knees, cradling my brother's head, both of them crying and apologizing.

I'm suddenly aware of my little arms, wrapped around Mom's big arm. My one cheek pressed to her bicep, the other vulnerable. One eye shielded by her skin, the other witnessing the eternal now.

BOTH

I show Joan an issue of *Hustler*. She nods. I slip the corner of the magazine just under the hem of her t-shirt. She slides it the rest of the way under.

She stands behind me at the doorway. The coast is clear. I dart the few steps to the bathroom and she follows.

The handles of the sink cabinet press circles on either side of my spine. Cold linoleum cools my bum. All the bath mat's tiny fingers press the backs of my calves. Joan locks the door.

As she settles in beside me, my fingers are already stroking the perfectly glossy skin of a woman. Her torso is nude above voluminous skirts. Will my breasts be as big as hers someday? She reclines amid dishevelled sheets on a pirate's berth. The pirate himself stands above her, arms akimbo. His white shirt is unlaced to the navel and the hem grazes a bulge, hidden beneath tight, mocha-coloured breeches. His thighs are taut as he ponders what to do with his wench. His captive. My gaze switches from slave to master, master to slave and back again.

"Do you think we'll meet pirates someday?" asks Joan.

Do I want to meet a pirate? Or be one? It never occurs to me that I could be both captor and captive. That I could want both a wench and a pirate.

My breath gusts in and out, chapping my lips. I slide my Lip Smacker out of my front pocket. It's thick enough to grip in a fist. Roughly, I rub some on. It tastes like bubble gum.

CARPACCIO

Mom and I ate raw meat. Beef, freshly-ground, or eye-of-round, sliced while frozen. Others gagged while we expressed our delectation around mouthfuls of chilled sweet cow.

From her, I learned to stab a wedge of lemon with a fork and squeeze against the tines. Olive oil must be drizzled first, to preserve the colour of the meat. Sometimes I forgot the order. Or pretended to forget. I wanted to blanche the bright flesh.

ORANGE PEEL

All I knew of my grandfather was the hollow place in the mattress of my grandmother's big bed, where I curled up and counted each breath by the tock of the grandfather clock until she came into the room, believing I was asleep.

She left the lamp on in the hall, the bedroom door ajar while she undressed. Through my barely open eye, I saw her big bra had two cups and only one cup was full.

She eased in beside me and her hollow chest and armpit zoomed into view. I shielded my new breasts, feeling her weight shift the mattress until morning.

Flying home aboard a Boeing, I glean words for Nonna's missing parts from an in-flight magazine. Breast cancer … its symptoms … "areola takes on texture of orange peel."

I inspect my brand new breasts in the lavatory mirror. Areolae puckered by cold air. Is that what orange peel looks like? Did I catch breast cancer from Nonna's sheets? Panic drips down my chest.

Me and my hypochondria, settling back into my seat. On the back of an airsickness bag I write: "Some hour, above Greenland, it all seems peaks. Flat mountain, land of no one, sea of snow. An archipelago of some supernatural body of liquid."

That fall, Mom gets the same diagnosis.

The hollow place in my hands expands like the Milky Way these days, rushing apart in every direction. When I lift both breasts into my big bra, I try not to feel anything but flesh.

CHEAT

First, the funicular from Brunate full of the usual commuters reaching the summit without breaking a sweat. What a cheat. Then, the raw meat thin as the terra cotta roof of Mom's old convent and clean as my writerly dreams. I was going on thirteen. Later, I would learn "cancer" but that day I was too young to notice we were sharing a rare day alone for a reason.

Barbecue

My dad stands in front of the grill, adjusting the flame. I slide open the patio door. The scent of crisping chicken skin and charring bone makes my mouth water.

"Can I sleep over at my friend's house?" I ask, expecting the usual rubber stamp. Instead, for the first time, he says no. This sudden withdrawal of freedom stuns me.

"Why not?"

He says I'm too old, I'm thirteen, I have "tits and everything." This is incomprehensible to me, a non sequitur. I protest his lack of trust.

"It's other people I don't trust," he says and turns a thigh, rearranges a rib.

Echolocation

The last campers left this morning, fingering necklaces of wolf-willow beads. They packed their buddy logs and mud-stained towels. They tied on friendship bracelets and began the roll home along gravel roads. Through the rising dust, we glimpsed their faces framed in rear windows, looking back at us. That last wave goodbye transformed us from counsellors back into exhausted teenagers planning a party.

Now the new moon hides among brilliant stars. Their shimmering echoes the tingle in my body, triggered by my first ride on the back of Alex's forbidden motorbike. His exhaust pipe branded me, sizzled a finger-long burn on my calf. At home, the blister will be proof of my disobedience. For now, I clasp the pain like a memento.

The open mouth of the sauna yawns like a starless patch of the same night sky. Alex walks toward it with two other couples. One of us laughs. I can barely make out Alex's crouch, his ducking head. I bend and follow him into the canvas-draped willow frame.

I feel my way along two long logs, lashed together to create a bench. Alex and I sit at the very back of the sauna on either side of the fire pit. The others are close beside us, three to a side.

Someone passes hot rocks in on a shovel. When Alex drops them into the pit. I taste a cloud of cold ash. He ladles water from the bucket and I listen for the familiar hiss of steam. Silence. The rocks are cold. We laugh and stay anyway.

We're hushed and warm in our huddle of skin. The sauna's willow-branch ribs flex behind my own. Someone passes me a bottle of crème de menthe. I take a swig. My knee presses against

an unseen, silken thigh. Scents intermingle. Willow and mint.
Lip gloss and chlorine residue. And then I feel my bathing suit top
stretching, pulled down by an invisible hand. The elastic catches
against my nipples then slides free. I discover my core, that epicentre of mouth-watering, instant swelling.

Catholic girl. Good girl. I know what I'm supposed to do.
Cover up. And I do.

But in the delightful, eternal pause before I sheath my skin,
another indelible discovery. Free in the cool air, my breasts can
sense the contours around me. They could guide me blind out of
caves, through dark woods, down coulee drops and up the rise of
cliffs. I would follow them all the way to myrrh-scented sand dunes
without stopping for water.

When I get home, it's to more bad news. Mom's breast cancer
is back. She won't last the year.

ZEST

Forget the usual method for grating the outermost peel. Forget the normal uses. My mother's recipe for making my eyes sparkle expressed a keener zest.

Drawing me in by cupping my chin, she would fold the skin of a peeled mandarin between thumb and finger, then press the waxy pores while aiming at my irises.

I'd glimpse a spray of droplets riding iridescent thread, like a sunstruck spiderweb after rain. Then flinch as my lids clenched, eyes stinging then opening to look up at her with glistening gaze. She'd touch her palms together once and step back and we would smile.

I knew that sting was coming every time but I kept my eyes wide open anyway. And when they laid her in the ground, I didn't blink.

Primi

THE ORCHARD

I awake feeling as if someone is calling me. Dad's snoring usually travels through doors and walls to every room of the house, but the house is quiet. I hear my clock ticking and turn in bed to read its glowing hands: two o'clock in the morning. I reach for my shawl and run my fingertips over the stitches, remembering how every millimetre of yarn ran through Mom's hands as she knit it for me. I wrap it around my shoulders, push my feet into sheepskin slippers then open the door. Down the hallway, my parents' bedside lamp glows. I walk toward the light.

Mom lies in the big bed, as she has since the day of my brother's wedding a month before. The blankets dip slightly on the side where her left breast once was. Her jaw is settled back slightly, making it seem she has an overbite, and her high cheekbones stand out as in her leaner youth. Her thin hair, carefully combed, looks accidental against the pillow. Her big, green eyes are open but immobile. Has it been only days since she's stopped tracking our movements? The nurse from the Victorian Order told us to expect this. As Mom gets nearer to death, she will appear to be asleep but we won't be able to wake her because she'll be in a coma.

I look across at Dad, who is sitting next to Mom on the bed. His close-set eyes seem closer together than ever. He's slept little for the last month, fearful of leaving Mom in pain by missing even one dose of painkillers. I know that hearing her in distress, he wakes to comfort her. He's told me she's been asking why it is taking so long to die. There are lay-offs in the oil patch, too, so he goes to work each day taut with the dread of losing his job. I pried into the Victorian Order of Nurses file last time they were here, so

I know they are watching out for him. They noted the number of espressos he has been drinking, among other concerns.

My parents' arguments still blaze vivid in my memory. Not long ago, I wondered if they were only staying together because of me, the last kid left at home. That made me feel guilty and resolve to grow up as quickly as possible. Now as I watch Dad caress Mom's cheek and whisper something to her in Italian, I wonder if I understand what love really means.

I haven't slept much myself. The other day, I fell asleep at school in front of my locker with my ear crushed against my Modern Biology textbook. I feel guilty about that, too. Unlike my dad, I'm not losing sleep nursing Mom. Instead I'm writing the last part of my story, "Indian Summer: The Season to Fall." I glance again at Mom. Her fixed gaze brings the first lines of my story to mind: "Miranda was half Cherokee and half blind. Her lifetime was more than half over. ... "

My mom's sister is sitting beside the bed. Her mood is hard to read, so I opt for kissing her on the cheek rather than saying anything.

"*Ciao, tesoro*," my aunt says softly.

Dad encourages her to go to bed. True, it *is* late and my *zia* has been there for hours despite jet-lag from her trans-Atlantic flight, but I sense an undercurrent of unease.

I know my mom's sister is exquisitely sensitive. Maybe their childhood had something to do with it.

She and Mom were raised in a convent in the foothills of the Italian Alps. Their mother, a travelling saleswoman raising them alone, felt her daughters would be safer there from the war. Though they escaped the worst of the air raids, the convent left other scars. Mom told me about kneeling on the stone floor of the cathedral until she fainted from pain and exhaustion. The nuns tied her left hand behind her back, insisting she become right-handed because the left hand was *sinistra*, the evil hand. If the children stained their hands or clothes when dipping nibs into inkwells, the nuns would make them dip their fingers into human feces as punishment. Parents would bring scarce items like powdered milk to the convent and the nuns would feast on it, while the children roamed the woods looking for berries and mushrooms to fill their empty bellies. Once, while scavenging, a girl fell into an uncapped, abandoned outhouse hole and nearly drowned in rotting excrement. Mom had railed at the injustice, incurring more severe punishment than the other children. Through it all, she protected her sister from the worst of the blows and held it together, the practical one who shielded her more vulnerable older sister.

Little wonder that Mom never mentioned God or went to church, and I am almost an atheist despite years of Catholic school. But still, she wanted the final sacrament. A priest performed Extreme Unction last week and the change in her was incredible. After weeks of feeling agitated and afraid, she became profoundly peaceful. What will do that for me, I wonder, when it's my time?

"*Dai*," Dad says to Zia, reassuring her that it is okay to go to bed. She relents, finally admitting fatigue.

"Wake me up as soon as something starts happening." She wants us to promise before she will leave, so we do, and she kisses her sister — so gently that lips and cheek barely touch.

I take the chair beside the bed, put a pillow on my lap and settle in with my best friend's graphic novel, *Ronin*. I flip through it, scanning superbly drawn images of bloody battles and murder. I stare at the page while my mind wanders back to my story.

"Miranda lives on her orchard with an acquaintance named Seth, who is impatiently awaiting her death. They both have no one, so she knows that he offers kindness only out of hope of inheriting her orchard. One day, she says her time is complete and asks Seth to help her end it ..."

I adjust the pillow in my lap and glance up at Mom. I should have been with her, or helping Dad instead of writing that story. But Mom knows I dream of being a writer. Ever since I wrote my first story on a manual Olivetti in grade five, she's known it. She always bought me books featuring characters who were writers, like *Little House on the Prairie* and *Are You There God? It's Me, Margaret.* And she brought me notebooks, *quaderni,* whenever she came home from Italy. I am used to grade school exercise books, manila covers bearing the Calgary Catholic School District logo in black ink. But those glossy, patterned and colourful *quaderni* seem to come from another planet entirely. Whether the pages are lined or unlined or graph paper, I fill up every one, feeling my dreams are bound to come true. That very year, she argued with over-protective Dad to allow me take my first writing workshop. And it turned out to be worth it. I finally wrote a good story. Mom would be happy for me, wouldn't she?

Over the past months, I began taking care of Mom. At first, she was outright mean to me. Maybe she was trying to protect me by pushing me away. But Mom is very proud and independent, so I figure she just wanted to do things for herself. Like Miranda did. "Miranda had enjoyed Seth at first. She was wise to his manoeuvres and often had to keep herself from laughing. And she loved to frustrate him by hanging on to her life for one more week, and then another and still another. But it was getting harder to enjoy Seth, with his smells of gasoline, beer and wet socks. As she lost the energy to work in the orchard, he was useful but no longer amusing. As the weeks went by, Miranda asked more and more of him. The thought of being dependent on a man like Seth made Miranda feel weak. It made her feel old. ..."

Eventually, Mom stopped resisting my presence. Dad wasn't sure at first whether it was wise to let me help, but wound up relenting, probably out of exhaustion. He made a point of doing the harder work himself, though, like helping her to the bathroom and later, onto the bedpan.

After school, while my friends hung out in the tire park, smoking while strategizing about how to get alcohol and lose their virginity, I took care of my forty-nine-year-old mom. I'd bring her *minestra*, spoon soup into her mouth and wipe her chin. Later, I'd make her a cup of *camomilla* and smooth *crema Nivea* on her chapped lips. Whenever one of us didn't feel well, she would always say, "*Metti cremina!*" or steep some tea for us. Nivea and chamomile are Mom's panaceas and I used them on her, hoping they would work.

Now, as I sit beside the bed, I wonder if Mom is glad to have me with her. I look up from the graphic novel, search her face for some expression. "*Guarda con gli occhi della mente*," Mom admonishes when I can't find something in the cupboards. Look with your mind's eye. But I still can't tell whether she even knows I am there.

Before long, her breathing gets very loud. I listen as if to a strange music. Each breath is a beat, and the pause between beats lengthens. Each breath comes with more effort, as though she needs every ounce of strength to complete this simple thing she's done unconsciously all of her life. It sounds like something is loose inside her chest. I imagine ribs suspended from strings, chiming together as the air rushes past them.

Dad whispers to Mom, then looks at me and says, "She's going." I put my fingers on her wrist, search for and find a weak pulse. The pause between breaths becomes so long, we think each is her last, but then another heaves through the silence, and we watch her face, and wait.

Finally, no other breaths come, and I feel the pulse in her wrist grow fainter. I feel it stop.

"I can't find a pulse," I tell Dad. I check again. Nothing.

I remember our promise to Zia. "I should go get her," I say, but Dad wants to clean up a little first, make the sight less shocking for her. So I wait. Too late now anyway.

Dad wipes Mom's mouth. Then draws her eyelids shut. One of them won't close. The day before, I wrote: "It was done. Seth stepped jauntily toward the half-ton truck. Its one remaining headlight stared at him so steadily, it could well have been Miranda's eye, the one that didn't close. It stared right at him, accusing him. Seth didn't care."

I sit motionless and emotionless. The seemingly prophetic nature of my words and an uncanny combination of facts combine to form a strange chant: One eye open. Three in the morning. Father's Day. I was born at 3 a.m.

Dad pulls aside the covers. I can't remember the last time I saw my mother in her underwear. Not long ago, she yanked down my blinds when she found me changing in front of the unshielded window. I still hear her admonishing me, "*Abbia un pò di pudore!*" – have some modesty. And now here I am, watching as Dad cleans and changes Mom into a fresh nightgown. I look away. One eye open. Three in the morning. Father's Day. Born at 3 a.m. "It's pretty simple, really, this death thing," I say to Dad. It seems real when people die on TV. But now I know it isn't, it isn't like on TV at all. Not full of action, not even a dramatic moment like in my story. Now I know the truth about death. A very quiet moment, very natural, so subtle you can miss it. One second a heart is beating and the next, it isn't. Between one pulse and another, a whole life is over. Everything you learned, everything you remember, all gone. Just like that. And I know the same will be true for me. I vow to live enough life for the both of us.

Once Dad is satisfied with how Mom looks, I go to my brother's old room, where Zia is sleeping. She's flown across the ocean to sit at her sister's deathbed, wanting to be there with her at the end. Now she's lost that too. I say her name before softly touching her shoulder but she still jumps. I search for words, borrow my Dad's "She's gone." Zia gets up in a flurry of blankets, swings on her robe, then rushes at me, hitting me feebly with her fists, shouting, "I told you to come get me, I told you!" I hold her up in my arms for a moment, feeling nothing. I follow her as she rushes down the hall.

Zia croons her sister's name through sobs. She begins smoothing the body's hair, caressing the cheek.

How weird. It's as if she believes she's talking to Mom, but Mom's not in there. Maybe that's what Zia's eyes know, why they are darting here and there on the landscape of Mom's face, over and over, searching for signs of her.

Dad asks me to call the funeral home. They have all the information, so I only have to notify them. I go downstairs to the kitchen and find the number on the corkboard.

Next to the phone, among other odds and ends, is the beautiful cloisonné box I bought for Mom. I meant it for her chemo pills. She flatly refused to use it. "They are pills, not candies," she said.

I fiddle with the box and listen to the dial tone while staring at the countertop. Suddenly, I see its white surface arrayed with our last haul of wild mushrooms, hear Mom's hoots of joy coming from somewhere through the trees as she discovers first one, then another choice edible for wild mushroom risotto or *funghi trifolati* ...

Finally, I dial the number.

"You've reached McInnis & Holloway. How can I help you?"

"Yes, um, hello. Um ... my mom is dead now."

"I'm sorry for your loss. Who's calling?"

"Meneghetti."

Next thing I know, a doctor arrives. He puts a stethoscope to the body's chest in several places, listening as though there is a chance he'll hear something. I laugh. I have already felt the silence he is hearing. His actions are a charade. He fills out paperwork certifying she is dead. "I could have told you that," I say. What's that look he gives me? Pity?

Then a procession of people come: it seems endless. All of them touching and talking to the body. I dismiss them as fools. Two men arrive carrying a black board and a purple blanket. Everyone else leaves, but I am curious to see everything. They lift Mom's corpse – for that's what it is now, isn't it? – onto the board. Once they arrange the blanket over her body, I rub the fabric between my thumb and forefinger. The inside of the blanket is cool and satiny. The outside is a warm velvet. Why would they put the velvety side *out* instead of *in*, against her skin? Oh. Because Mom is dead. The blanket isn't meant to soothe her. It's meant for us.

I follow the undertakers out the front door. The hearse is parked beneath our big poplar tree. How can the leaves look yellow when I smell the fresh fragrance of bright June green? What's wrong with me?

When the men open the back doors, the grey satin valences on the back windows swing slightly. Once they slide the board onto the grey-carpeted interior, I turn and walk back up the driveway and into the kitchen.

I see Mom sweeping the kitchen floor in her housedress, as she has every day for as long as I can remember. An Italian cassette is playing, the one that Zia sent, and Mom is singing along.

After this life that forgets you,
After this sky without a rainbow
After this melancholy, these lies

After all this longing for peace
Tell me, who will there be?

Suddenly, she inhales sharply, bracing herself against the table. The cancer has spread to her liver and any bending motion causes terrible pain. I try to take the broom from her, but she yanks it back. We both stand alone, crying.

There will be
A shadow at your side, dressed in white
There will be
A kinder way to say, "I love you."

My sister's voice pulls me away from my memory.

"I guess this is our job now," she says, unloading the dishwasher.

"Actually, it's been our job for a while already," I say, opening the cutlery drawer and taking a handful of spoons from her. Their shiny curves nestle together in the tray. I find it comforting.

I bend over and shake my hair, tossing it back as I straighten. Got to look good. If my name is called for the Grade 11 English Award, I will be up on stage in front of the whole school. I turn sideways and look at my belly in the mirror. Good. It's not sticking out very far today. I hear the garburetor-like sound of the garage door lifting; my cue that Dad's ready to leave. I take one last look in the mirror and rush down the stairs and out to the car.

The passenger seat is empty. Otherwise, everything's the same. My sister sitting beside me in the back seat. Dad chain-smoking Rothmans king-sized with the windows sealed shut "so the air conditioning works." The slipped disc in his back causing an uneven pressure on the gas pedal so that the car lurches forward and lags back, forward and back, making me feel carsick, as usual.

The linoleum floors of my high school shine with new polish. Dad, my sister and I walk past the award cases lining the entrance hall. I've seen them day after day for the past two years, but now the cases seem larger, fuller. Will my name be engraved on one of the trophies for all to see, now and in coming years? My stomach flutters. But Dad and my sister don't seem excited. Of course not. Mom died just a few days ago. What kind of daughter could care about an award at a time like this? But I do.

Being at school after supper is strange. The deserted halls seem longer, narrower. Unopened lockers line the walls like tiles and their silver locks are like the identical links of a chain.

It's a relief to get to the gym, which is alive with students, teachers and parents. The sliding panels on the far wall of the gym are open to the stage. Drama students are checking the stage lights, and the heavy velvet curtains are pulled aside to reveal the black floor and scrim. Chairs are set up in rows, leaving a runway down the centre for the award-winners to approach the stage.

My sister and I both look up at the stage. "I feel pretteeee, oh so pretteeee," she sings half-heartedly. I bat my lashes, clasp my hands together beside my cheek and reply, "I feel prettee and witteee and briiiight, and I piteee any girl who isn't meeee tooonight!" We chuckle a bit, remembering the *Westside Story* production she danced in on this stage a few years ago.

I spot one of the popular kids. Her sleek, blonde hair is perfect and her corduroys must be a size one. If only I win the award! That'll show her. I fiddle with my belt, making sure my shirt's tucked in flat over my belly.

Mr. Bedard, the teacher who made me work hard on my stories for the first time, smiles at me from across the gym. My English teacher, Mr. MacIlhone, waves at me from the stage. A good sign?

My stomach flutters again. No, they're probably just being extra nice because of what happened.

Dad finds some seats and we settle into them. I try to pay attention while the other awards are presented so I can clap at the right times. Then, finally, the English awards start. I'm excited, but Dad's distracted, looking down at his palms. Is he falling asleep? My sister's in her own world, too. I fix my hair and wonder why I'm not sad, like them. I should be, shouldn't I? Is there something wrong with me?

"I was blessed with a gifted group of young people this year," says Mr. MacIlhone. "And one of those students has earned this year's English Award." So! It's going to be someone from my class! Maybe that cutie who loves the Doors and writes those sci-fi stories?

"Congratulations to ... Monica Meneghetti! Come on up here and get your trophy."

In a daze, I slide out to the aisle and start walking toward the stage. The gym floor is waxy and my shoes stick to it a little. Looking down at my feet, I see fragmented lines in red, black, green, blue, and it takes me a moment to realize they are basketball court lines, criss-crossing the aisle. I jog up the stairs to the stage, hoping my boobs don't bounce too much. And then I'm beside Mr. MacIlhone hoping I don't look fat, and he's waiting for me to shake his hand. Beside him is Mr. Bedard, holding a huge trophy that gleams white and gold. Handing it to me he says, "Your name will be engraved on it later this week," and winks. Somehow, it doesn't feel as great as I imagined. I stand with them both, smile my best smile for the camera. Then they take the trophy away, into the wings.

Back at the seats, no one seems happy for me. Dad is wiping his eyes with a tissue. My sister tidies her mascara with an index finger. I stare at the bouquet of white roses in my arms, wondering how they got there. Wondering who will buy me notebooks now.

In the car, I hear a female voice: "*Ti piaciono le rose?*" Do I like the roses. The words seem to be coming from where Mom usually sits. Confused, I look up. Zia is looking back at me from the passenger seat. Why hadn't I seen her there before? They're from mamma, she tells me. She would be so proud of you.

Dad lurches the car toward home. I'm not sure I like roses.

Beached

My aunts unfold beach chairs on the tidal flat. They call me *piccola*, little one, then tell me *Ormai sei una donna,* you're already a woman. Your *mamma* would be proud.

I can't remember, or have chosen to forget, the years when I had a mother. It seems I never had a mother at all.

While the two of them start planning a birthday dinner for my twentieth, I take a walk.

Shadow planets orbit the poles of beach umbrellas, just as they once did. My sister and I once abandoned that sheltered world of shadow and ran to the sea.

Our feet swam in grey sand. Each grain was a burning ember. We snatched our steps all the way to the border, to the place where fine, grey heat meets a firm, damp expanse of chestnut-coloured sand. *Ragazzi* played *calcio* on the rippled surface. Their soccer ball tumbled from crest to crest of the tidal flat's miniature dunes, frolicking between allegiances.

Little creatures scrabbled out from under our feet. We squatted to touch the spiral and cone shells of *granchioline.* Their tiny legs peeked out like toes from the hole in a sock. Small holes in the sand reminded us how a straightened coat hanger could fish a long, flat shell out from down below. The creature would sense intrusion and clamp on, only to be exposed and suspended in sunlight.

The hand of a tidal flat stretched far, as far as it must to stay connected to the sea.

The shallow water was warm. Our toes grasped the sand as waves pushed against our legs. Chest deep, arms above the surface, we twisted from side to side as we walked forward. Our feet squished suddenly, sinking into slime. It was warm and deep, who knew how deep. The slime had fingers. Thrilled and disgusted, we shrieked "*Melma! Melma!*" as we hopped and breaststroked away, letting the sea rinse away tendrils of ooze until we dared to touch bottom again.

Mom draped a warm towel over my cool, wet skin. It felt like being swathed in sunshine. Her arm embraced and braced my back while she tugged my wet bathing suit bottoms down. My body wobbled with her tugging. Naked now but for sand socks, hand on her shoulder for balance, I aimed for the leg holes of a dry bathing suit.

None of the moms let their kids sit in wet bathing suits. *Si deve cambiare.* A wet bathing suit is an evil magnet for sickness and infection. It had to be changed. Kids with colds mustn't expose their shoulders on the *spiaggia*. Woollen sweaters mandatory; bare legs permitted. Sick kids must sweat beneath fibres laden with sandcastles and salt.

Mothers on other umbrella planets were stuffing chunks of chocolate into fresh buns. Kids clutched their snacks. Within the bread glaring white as nebulae in their fists, chocolate melted into black holes.

A full belly mustn't touch water. Swimming after eating is asking for trouble, for cramps or drowning. Two hours' wait was the talisman. *Si deve aspettare.*

Meanwhile, the megaphone blared. *Attenzione, attenzione!* Such and such a child is lost on the beach. *Achtung, achtung!* The same child was lost in German. Dad made his mock announcement. "*Einen kleinen* pistul-inen is lost-en on the beach-en again-en!"

I held my waiting like an amulet.

Zio's hairy belly bulged out like mine. I pushed a finger into it. He grabbed my hand and laughed. In his sunglasses, there were two of me.

Where's your *umbellico*? All the other girls have belly buttons, he said. I looked around the beach. He was right. Belly buttons winked from high above bikini bottoms. I looked down and saw only the bare skin of my stomach above waist-high bathing suit bottoms. Where was my *umbellico*?

Ah! he said, bumping the side of his head with the heel of his hand. You must have lost it.

Eyes wide, I scouted the sand. He helped me rummage around, sifting grains through his fingers. Found it! He stuck it back on. That was close, he said. You better keep an eye on it.

Now, the chestnut-coloured sand is dormant. Not a single tickle beneath my feet. I miss the little shells. But the hand of a tidal flat still stretches far, as far as it must.

My aunts are still on their beach chairs, laughing and gesticulating. Mussels for your birthday, *piccola*. What do you think?

Flesh

A net full of mussels dangles from the chocolate-tan fingers of my aunt's hands. The shellfish drip a trail of salt-water onto the cobblestones, all the way to the seaside apartment that she shares with my father's youngest brother. Walking down this ancient street, I slowly recover from the shock of resembling the woman I've been unable to mourn.

I turned thirteen the last time I was in Italy. Now, here in a beach town on the Adriatic Sea, I will turn twenty over a meal of *cozze*.

My aunts and uncles had greeted me on platforms or arrival gates. They'd enfolded me in festive, chattery hugs. While relishing their embraces, I was shielded from their frank gazes. But once a *zio* stepped back to lift a suitcase or a *zia* released me to another's greeting, their eyes widened and their mouths dropped open in wonder, a tear or two slipping free as they looked and looked at me. They looked, not because I had left a child and returned a woman, but because their sister had last said goodbye to them in her middle age and they wouldn't see her again, except in her daughter's close resemblance. They looked because they'd missed her Canadian funeral, because they inhabited an illusion created by my face: my mom, still alive, still twenty years old.

The *cozze* are poems, each dark oval needing much care before being coaxed to open. My *zia* places the bundle into her kitchen's stainless steel sink. The sound of shell against metal makes me suddenly aware of how hard *cozze* are. I'd forgotten their secretive carapaces, thinking only of the yielding, salmon-coloured flesh. Now, for only a moment, I hear the grit of sand caught between shell and sink, the white barnacles setting their serrated edges against steel.

We set to work. Bangles slide down her forearm as she lifts a glass of *aperitivo* then drop back down when she picks up the knife to scrape the shells. As her hands move, I watch the golden circlets briefly separate from each other, inevitably reuniting in music.

Cozze. How lovely, how strange. I heard the word for the first time this morning. Dad called them *peoci*. My brother, sister and I called them "black dock-stickers" because they clung along the docks at our beach, scraping our thighs when we wiggled breathlessly out of the sea onto the warm wood.

As I rest my grip from the task of scraping shells, Zia fills a deep pot with water. When she smiles at me, it's easy to imagine she's Egyptian or Ethiopian. I grew up in Canada. My pale skin burns and peels before grudgingly offering up a tan that quickly fades beneath a feather-filled parka.

When Zia says the word *cozze*, the deepness of her voice matches her skin's hue as though the tanning has tuned her voice, bronzing her speech from alto toward tenor. And then, there's her mouth. Her words always slip past precisely the right lipstick named after floral shades not found in Canadian gardens, colours that perfectly coordinate with her blouses or bikinis, that seem to polish her green irises and make me wonder if she has flecks of actual emeralds in her eyes. Each time I say this new word – *cozze, cozze* – I become tinted with her mystique.

My dad's sister arrives – kiss-kiss – wearing a bright yellow, raw silk dress, and promptly scolds us for not opening the patio doors. I watch her stride across the living room, relieved not to see her naked bum. I am staying with her. Yesterday, she stirred pasta sauce, clad only in an apron. The day before, she sorted laundry in the nude.

She pulls the first glass door aside, and then the next and the next, until the entire wall of the living room is gone, until the living room seems to stretch out past the television, past the chaise longues and potted plants, along the ceramic patio tiles, until finally it seems you could dive straight into the sea. I had seen the rows of door buzzers in the courtyard, had walked among the crowds of people strolling the boardwalk between the apartment complexes and the sea. But right now, the architect's illusion prevails. "Feels as though we're on the deck of a ship, alone at sea," I tell her. "*Ecco, esatto*," she says.

Zia leans in and speaks sotto voce: "There's something you need to understand about your mamma." She looks not at me, but into me. Like my dad, she has close-set, small eyes. Her long, narrow nose seems to focus her gaze, as though she were taking a photo of me through a zoom lens. My mouth is dry but I go through the reflex of swallowing anyway.

"Some think your mamma was a hard woman. Cold. But I knew her differently. She confided in me. Actually, she was very sensitive. She loved everyone, she gave herself to them, she loved the world. That's who she really was."

I recall the exquisitely smooth skin of mamma's arm. After dinner, she in her chair, me in mine, I would lean against her, wrap both of my little arms around her one big arm, and stay there, my cheek pressed to her bicep, stroking her skin right there at the kitchen table. We never tired of it, never felt awkward about it, even in my teens.

But our peaceful oasis also weathered droughts. She would discover the lid left off of the jam jar — "*Ancora!*" — and I would flee from her bilious rage into the yard, the lake, or my diary.

"I guess I can sort of see it," I tell my aunt. She pinches my cheek between her thumb and the knuckle of her curled forefinger, jiggling the flesh slightly back and forth for a moment. "*Che bella, che bella*," she sings out, and from the kitchen my other aunt exclaims, "*Bellissima!*"

The scent of steaming *cozze* drifts out to us along with that tenor voice. The marine breeze rustles the curtains, furled like sails at the edges of what remains of the living room wall, and we let the breeze carry us back to the kitchen. Over the counter, Zia hands me food to put on the table: *olio d'oliva*, sliced *pomodori, pane, insalata*.

One by one, uncles and cousins join us at the table. We begin to speak all at once, conversations overlapping, jousting, everyone striving to dazzle with their eloquence so they can claim a moment of full attention on their own story, their own voice, before someone else's passionate words surge over everyone, until the next wave breaks, and all the while, bowls fill, bread tears from the loaf, wine splashes into tumblers and empty shells clink against porcelain.

I place some steamed *cozze* into my bowl. Like books left ajar, their shells now allow glimpses of private life. I lift the shells one by one to my mouth, careful not to spill their liquid, and work the meat out with my teeth and tongue. Or I pull the pinkish-orange ovals free with my fingers, pausing to notice how smooth their flesh is, and how much smaller the creature than the shell it inhabits.

SECRET INGREDIENTS

Within the *risotto* lurks the texture of being loved. History's *al dente* stands at the centre, surrounded by the long-simmered softness of forgetting. Saffron scent blossoms into belonging.

Layered within smooth-as-skin pasta, the *ragù* of resentment mingles with the *besciamella* of abandonment. Melted mozzarella blankets *lasagne* like longing.

Sage infuses drawn butter with dusty grief, the only way to swallow the joy of *gnocchi*.

WATER

Twenty years old and backpacking above tree-line on a hot day. We must be impatient to lose our sweat.

Not just today but for years we've been thirsty and it's no wonder, sipping as we have been from random springs. Catholic virgins, we've tried almost every other kind of elixir. Seems we've waited a long time to drink. Perhaps you've abandoned hope. Meanwhile, this water has taken centuries to fill this river.

Now I make you carry your life on your back, exposed to mammoth ice, cliffs, wind, moon, claws before I surprise you. Blisters, knotted shoulders and sunburn are the price of our quenching.

I show you the condoms. We need the instructions but I didn't bring a flashlight. We read them by the glow of the lighter you keep tucked inside your Player's Light. Careful not to melt the translucent dome of nylon above our heads.

Did the Little Yoho River pause when I first welcomed you inside me? I know I felt its buck and swirl. My body flowed as right as a swelling river at spring run-off. I felt you treading water in that current.

The next night, zipped into our separate sleeping bags, you asked the alpine air, "Does this mean we have to get married?" I said no.

We went home and got even better at doing it than we'd been on the first try. Paranoid about pregnancy, I went on the pill. My emotions became volatile. A few months later, you said you couldn't handle my moods and broke up with me. I sat pounding the steering wheel of my Chevette with my fists. Maybe they were right: you didn't want to buy the cow.

SALAD

The plan with Toby was to go dancing with some friends. We made it as far as the parking lot.

At the passenger door of my silver Chevette, we kissed our first kiss while my key was still turning in the lock. Toby got in and I straddled him. My fingers tangled in his crazy curls and my thighs clenched his taut cyclist's legs. Even with all of our clothes on, a sudden mist rolled in and steamed up the windows. His lips might as well have been a bong because suddenly I was not sober enough to drive. I must have steered through a gauntlet of traffic violations. If side-swiping torsos, colliding bodies and speeding pulses could earn citations, my glove box would have sprung open under the pressure of accumulated tickets. The Chevette made it to his apartment without a scratch. I, on the other hand, did not.

Toby spread a quilt on the worn shag carpet and put Grateful Dead on the stereo. He kicked the leather sandals off of his sturdy wide feet and shucked the Guatemalan woven cotton clothes to reveal his solid, stocky body. Behind large, wire-rimmed glasses, his eyes were pale blue and wild. When he smiled, it seemed his mouth was watering. Within moments, I was naked and dancing.

He was the first lover with whom I experienced that intoxicating, random thing called chemistry. Between dates, I would lie on my bed in the afternoon and listen to the mix tape he'd made for me. "Astral Weeks," "Madame George," "Aerial Boundaries," "Ripple" live. I didn't need to imagine him, or what we'd done together. Just a few bars of sound was enough to turn me on. It was my first aural sex.

So you see why I easily gave up homemade *pasta alle vongole* to sit in Toby's spartan kitchen at a third-hand Arborite table and munch on nothing but unseasoned steamed broccoli.

His roommate that year was a Japanese exchange student whom Toby loved to tease with his bawdy sense of humour. My favourite line of his was, "Did you find someone to play your *shakuhachi* yet?" That one would make the shy guy blush and say "sayonara."

Toby's fridge was the hybrid of a health freak's paradise and a poor student's larder. Once, I flipped open the butter compartment and found only a tiny tin-foil package the size of a Tylenol. I had never seen a tab of LSD before. When I figured it out, months later, we argued.

"How can you play with your brain chemistry like that?"

"Everything changes your brain chemistry. Candy. Coffee. Kissing." He paused and smiled that mouth-watering smile of his. "Why is this different?" He ranted about the chemical soup of life and piercing the veil, then gave me Aldous Huxley's *The Doors of Perception.* I read it while he practised guitar. He played Needle and the Damage Done and sang almost like Neil Young.

I moved into residence for the last semester of my BA. Our floor was known as the Morgue. Only serious nerds wound up there. Across the hall from me lived a brainy, cycle-racing Adonis. He was reluctant to shave his legs for the upcoming race, so a hot mathematician and a goth actress got him astonishingly, incapacitatingly drunk. Once he was passed out, they shaved him from toe to groin. Over the next few weeks, as the hair grew back in, he'd scratch himself and swear, "It feels like my balls are in an iron maiden."

On the single bed of my private room, Toby made sleeping over into a euphemism. We lost ourselves in Enya and Cowboy

Junkies and tried not to get any body parts jammed into the electrical socket near the mattress.

The floor supervisor lived beside me. When I graduated, he gave everyone who was moving out a certificate. He'd made up cute nicknames for everyone. Mine was "Squeaky Bed." I was shocked. He said, "Are you kidding me? You didn't know the electrical sockets are like megaphones around here?"

I lived with Toby for a little while after leaving res, trying to decide what to do next. He talked about doing some aid work in Africa before starting grad school and asked me to go with him. I was scared. I'd only ever travelled to Italy and had left home only six months earlier. For the first time in my life, I was broke. Leaving home earlier than traditionally expected had left my relationship with my strict, old-world father in ruins, along with my confidence.

Toby seemed used to poverty and rootlessness. He dreamed of aimlessly road-tripping in a VW van. When he talked about it, I imagined a woman-shaped cut-out occupying the passenger seat of his imagination, a scripted role he wanted me to fill. I was a geeky Italian girl raised by an Italian Catholic father and convent-raised mother. It would take more than a few tokes to turn me into the footloose hippie he wanted. Besides, I preferred the driver's seat.

When I said Toby was a poor student, that might have been an understatement. After tuition and rent, not much was left for food. He hoarded condiment packets from the university's food court. When he made toast, he scrutinized the bread for mould first.

I was always hungry at his place, in more ways than one. My desire for him was swiftly aroused and intense but hardly ever satisfied. I was too naïve and guilt-ridden about pleasure to ask him to keep going, to find more ways to satisfy me. I glimpsed the fathomless nature of my desire but wasn't ready to accept it.

One night, he served me a huge plate of salad drenched in dressing, a welcome change from his usual steamed veg with plain brown rice. I dug in, humming "tasty" around half-masticated leaves. My Mediterranean tongue soaked the olive oil in as if the appreciation of extra-virgin were genetic. I licked balsamic vinaigrette from the corners of my grin. Every so often, he would stop eating and smile that mouth-watering smile of his while he watched me fork vegetables into my mouth. When I was finished, he handed me a slice of bread to mop up the leftover dressing. The bread was a little stale but I was still hungry.

I was wiping my mouth on my sleeve when he said, "Tonight's dinner, courtesy the Safeway dumpster. Can you believe they *threw* that stuff *out*?"

ROAR

The first time my writing dreams disgorged me, I found myself
sealed behind shatter-proof glass on the some-teenth floor of an
oil-patch office tower, where I tried not to needlessly swivel my
ergonomic chair. I acquiesced to the lady-like clothing my mom had
always wanted me to wear but drew the line at pantyhose, nailpolish
and make-up.

My three-drawer desk was in the realm of remote sensing. It
was a kingdom without queens, where lords summoned ladies when
the coffee pot was empty and ladies with legs stuffed into nylon
casings grumbled but still measured out the grounds. Clients called
me with coordinates. A satellite captured the images. I ordered and
shipped them.

At five o'clock, the C-Train took me home to my boyfriend.
"From above, Earth is an impressionist painting," I told him. And
then went into the kitchen.

We had a deal. I'd try to pace the linoleum floor wearing
six-inch heels; he'd give me a foot massage. The shoes were black
patent leather with gold stilettos. I could hardly stand up in them.
Maybe that was the point.

The shoes didn't do much for me. The lingerie he bought
me was another story. I'd always eschewed feminine clothing,
but now, garters and Cuban-heeled stockings, lace panties and
micro mini-skirts stoked my lust. To my dismay, I began coveting
corsets.

Seeing myself in the mirror, the air-brushed images I'd seen
in my early porn mag years ghosted before my eyes as though I'd
looked too long into the sun. Was I colluding with the oppression

of women? Could I still call myself a feminist? Should I stop wearing these clothes, sacrifice my own pleasure on political grounds?

Meanwhile, my friend Fay was having an affair with her boyfriend's sister. I had watched her vivid lips form the words but the sound of her voice was soon engulfed by the surf pounding in my ears. Walking home, the street seemed to telescope ahead of me. The front door receded from my approach.

"Are you okay?" my boyfriend asked.

"Fay just told me she's in love with a woman."

"Oh. How do you feel about that?" He waited.

"Strange. I just realized I've been attracted to her all along."

"Well, that's interesting ... What will you do about it?"

"Nothing. We're engaged."

"Perhaps you should explore this a little, before we get married ..."

"Of course not. That would be cheating."

I had a secret office ritual in those days.

I would keep my pants around my ankles, just in case someone looked under the door of my bathroom stall. I didn't want anyone getting suspicious.

Then I'd unwrap my third Coffee Crisp of the day. Prying the wafer layers apart with my incisors was as much a part of the ritual as my disappointment with the coffee cream. It was too weak. Every time.

The parted curtain of my hair hid my hands as they fed me. Even from above, you couldn't see the chocolatey coating disappearing into my mouth or the discarded yellow wrapper disappearing into the wall bin marked "feminine napkins." No one could see the evidence.

My mom always hid chocolate bars from us. I found them easily. And stole them. Candies she kept out of reach in the top cupboard, in a terra cotta dish with a black-glazed etching at the bottom. Pies, cakes and cookies were scarce. If she ever baked, she would use every trace of batter in the bowl. Wielded by my mom, a spatula was every bit as thorough as a child's tongue.

I would spend my entire allowance on Big Chief beef jerky and Hot Rods, on Twizzlers, Ton o' Grape gum and licorice pipes, on Sweet Tarts and Pop Rocks and Sherbet Fountains. And still, I would have room for more.

I looked out my office window one day, down onto the roof of the Hotel Regis. And there it was: a lion the colour of sunstruck wheat. The beast lay in a torpor, so still and stretched, it might have been a rug. Businessmen strode along the sidewalk as usual, oblivious to the claws above their busy brains. They walked with purpose, confidently wearing shoes made from the skin of prey.

The lion sensed me looking down at him, at his imprisonment without walls, at his belly fur matted by drainage pebbles instead of savanna. We locked eyes for a second — his the colour of my clandestine wrappers and nestled just as close to blood — and in that tick of time, my heart coiled up as my brain marshalled muscles to flee. But something lingered in his eye, a mote of his lost kingdom. He raised his muzzle as though to catch the scent of his pride within the city's fumes. And then he looked away and I looked away, too, knowing he didn't want any witnesses either.

The lion turned out to be part of Jungle Jane's ménagerie. Her exotic dance was on every night that week. There was a whole semi-trailer full of animals parked behind the Regis. Boas. Tarantulas.

It was impossible not to imagine the serpent muscle coiled around her naked skin, warm and dry and reassuring as the squeeze of a friend's hand. The spider's hairs, as scratchy as five-o'clock shadow against her breasts and quivering with the woofers' bass notes. The spotlights illuminating the individual curls of her teased coiffe. Spinnerets exuding silk under the strobes. The lion, striding onto the proscenium and stroking against her thigh like a tomcat.

I've loved snakes ever since the pet store clerk in our neighbourhood mall let me hold a baby boa. I must have been about fifteen because I remember begging Mom to let me buy it while my sister threatened to move into the garage if she said yes. But I couldn't get over that boa. How it wrapped itself like a living rope of leather around my forearm and held me tight. How it extended about twelve inches of its length into thin air, as if a tightrope and its walker had fused and forgotten safety nets entirely. Even stretched out like that and jutting at right angles to my arm, the snake's head held steady. What infinitely flexible strength! I began to covet that sort of strength. The longer I held the boa, the more I absorbed its power. That is why little girls are taught to dislike snakes.

After I found out about Jungle Jane, I pulled open my desk drawer and reached into my candy bar stash. My fourth Coffee Crisp, smuggled up my sleeve. Before heading to the washroom, I looked across the street at the roof of the Regis. The lion must have been drugged. How else could such a wild thing not rile and roar?

Water Closet

She insists on calling me her roommate. And the fortunate acoustics of my closet *do* bring her into my room – the sound of her in the shower, the sound of water falling onto her, into my room. I hold my breath, push dirty laundry aside and enter my confessional. I hear water, tapping a rhythm on her skin with so many fingertips. Her body squeaking against the tub as she lays down on the porcelain.

She's shown me this before. I know what comes next.

The droplets change in tone as she turns the dial to a stream-ing arc, thudding into her. A deliberate wetness.

I hold my breath, try to hear past my heart for fear I'll miss her voice: at first a random sound, as though clearing her throat and then ... the pulsing aria. My heart beats in more than one place.

She would have me stay in this closet forever. And she would be ever so clean.

Nearly the First

There. Beneath the swinging vertical blind. That ray of sunlight. It gilds the room. Rhythmic clicking as the slats collide.

Such a slow afternoon, so full of laughter. Then so suddenly serious, when she asks to take a nap with me. So suddenly careful, when we try to lie side by side without touching.

I have already seen her – in the shower, head turned, face away from me – I have already heard her pleasure – the melody of sung sighs over the backbeat of water droplets – but I have never touched her skin.

Now suddenly, skin. A fine, unfamiliar fabric of pores stretching over breasts and folding over belly and tucking below buttocks. She lies down and turns her back to me. Her back. I reach out then pause, somehow afraid my fingers will leave marks on her. My hand on her skin, so suddenly slow, so infinitesimally slow. There seems so much of her, and my hand, so small to cover all. But one hand is all I allow myself.

Suddenly, she stops me. I can't remember when, was it here? My fingers curling the curls of her mound? Or my lips encircling her areola, my tongue wet on inverted nipple?

I can't ignore my desire. She hasn't yet seen me nude. She hasn't yet heard my pleasure. She still will not touch me. But now she sees and hears me touch myself.

We never spoke of this.

Nor did it happen again.

Opening Up

"Can bisexuals be monogamous?" I email CJ. She's the only bisexual I know. Four hundred kilometres away from my small town.

"Of course. Some are, some aren't. The real question is, are you?"

Sheldon and I U-Hauled it after three months. Three years in, and I don't see an end to it. Don't want to. Does this mean I'll never have a girlfriend?

"I can't answer that for you," Sheldon says. "Let me know when you figure it out."

By the time Sheldon and I fell in love, we both knew I was into women as well as men. Neither of us gave any thought to how it might play out in our relationship. Until now.

CJ advises via email: Is my desire and curiosity for women strong enough that I might wind up in bed despite my best intentions?

It could happen. I haven't had a chance to fully experience women yet. The one three-way I have had is not nearly enough, and given my passionate, curious nature, a lapse is possible.

Probably best to face this head on then, writes CJ. Come to an agreement now, so you don't betray someone you love. Someone you want to have in your life indefinitely. You wouldn't want to hurt him like that.

A few months later, I risk reading my Sapphic writing at someone's art party. I'm nervous. Since they always see me holding hands with Sheldon, likely everyone assumes I'm straight.

I reassure myself before reading. People won't assume it's about me. It's poetry, so they won't automatically think it's true ...

But right after the party, two women approach me.

"Hot poem," says the one with long dark hair. She introduces herself.

At first, Rachel puts the poem and my short, spikey hair together and takes me for a lesbian. Then, after seeing me with Sheldon on the street, she realizes I am bisexual, like her, and comes out to me. Now I know two bisexuals in total. And I'm not the only one in town after all.

Several years from now, she will be the first woman whose hand I hold. The delicacy of her hand in mine will astonish me. She will say, "This is what a woman's hand feels like." And I will say, "Actually, it feels a lot like my ex-husband's." She will use those agile fingers to coax an orgasm from me in a public place while outside the window, fluffy snowflakes fall through the five points of a buck's antlers. As I catch my breath, she will laugh and say, "Congratulations. You're officially bi."

But for now, we will talk and talk about sex, about what it means to be bisexual. For several months, she tells me what she knows about alternative relationships. Then after giving me a book on open relationships, she leaves town, as so many do.

Leaving me to ponder the question once again: Can I forego the possibility of female partners? After those months of talking with Rachel, after almost a year of considering it, I know my answer. But I am scared to tell Sheldon. Will he be able to handle this, or will I lose a potential life partner? I am not prepared for that possibility. Still, it exists. But I don't want anything to come between us. If our love is to continue, let it proceed honestly.

Heart pounding, I sip my glass of water. Put it down. Pick it up and gulp it all down. "I can't go the rest of my life without expressing this part of my sexuality," I say. "But I still want to be with you. I don't know what to do."

He says, "Let's open our relationship then. Women only."
And so, we do.
It doesn't occur to me to ask, "Define *women*."

BOREAL

I leave the entryway, door half-shut behind, sway blindly between kitchen and hearth, eyes adjusting to the dark of this house.

Porchlight leaks through curtained glass, sketches a gesture of you, swell of hip thrust back bending to cold stone, hair sparking tinder against cheek. You rise from the hearth to greet me. You do not carry fire: your hands themselves are aflame.

I snuff your fingers one by one against my tongue, they sizzle, pinched. Your palms hang smoke in the moonlight, smudge charcoal in my hair, they ride your arms hard, bareback to the hearth. Glowing wood tantalizes your hands. The drama of combustion makes you bend again, your hands penetrate heat, emerge as coals, shift orange/black toward me across lifelines of magma.

Are you looking up at me or have I grown? Even on tiptoe in front of you, I fail to retrieve my pulse now chiming the kitchen's spent chandelier.

Your face is a triangle connecting eye, eye, chin and within this polygon, a blushing tripod swells, corner, corner, bottom lip. Let go, "let go," only to wrap closer, tighter to the dip.

Your glowing hands shoot like stars across a sky innocent of aurora. Their trajectory allows the tongue time to exclaim, but the eye is never certain anything was seen.

Later, I will act as if it is Wednesday though the calendar says Thursday. Then, we'll have use for nouns, for countdowns. I will try to ignore the warm, pink fossil I carry in my mouth.

Rice-Cooker Porridge

In her basement on Queen Street East, below the low ceiling, amid the glow of mini-lites, within windowless walls hung with torn paper pierced and joined by porcupine quills, in the bed that is not my bed that is not her bed but the bed in which she sleeps, I wake up.

A passing streetcar vibrates torn paper.

She ducks her head through the doorframe. In her hands, a bowl of oatmeal. In her tanning-leather hands, her plucking-gut and sewing-moccasins hands, her stringing-beads-and-long-bows hands, her resting-on-my-wool-clad-thigh-making-me-squirm-for-skin hands, in those hands that oatmeal.

The oatmeal made in a rice cooker, the cooker on the counter of the kitchen. The kitchen that is a hallway with bar fridge, hot plate and cutting board, the "L" shaped hallway with a counter for a kitchen table.

Upstairs is a wide, bare floor and a wall of mirrors. Upstairs, where yesterday we sat facing each other — she on a chair cradling a guitar and me on the floor leaning against a wall opposite the mirror, the mirror reflecting her and myself back to me — I sat writing. How did I write while she sang a song of cracks, crevasses, fragments? The chasm between us since the night before.

The night before, I lay awake as she slept beside me in the same but different bed. My bed: a cloud of whispers and want, my wont to want to be inside her. Her bed but a spring-loaded launch pad. I marinated in want while she snored. Like some '80s pop song, I wanted her to want me.

But the porridge. What about the porridge?

She'd been married once, back when she still appeared to

be a man, to a Scottish woman who found sweet oatmeal silly. Her ex-wife liked her porridge salty, as it was meant to be. Brown sugar, nuts and dried currants? What a farce. She cooks sweet oatmeal porridge for me anyway.

The passing streetcar vibrates torn paper.

She stoops to bring me breakfast in that bed where my body stretches and my hope yawns. She serves me porridge as though coaxing a wounded animal from its burrow. Provides nourishment as though she held me precious. Tenderness blazes like a corona around the totality of her scars.

She offers me oatmeal. Her fingernails click on the bowl. Those fingernails she dips in contact cement and acrylic powder, layering them until five guitar picks tip the fingers of her right hand, the hand devoted to frets and fletches. She is always careful, if ever she strums me, to strum me with her other hand.

I eat my porridge. My lip bleeds. The cold sore on my lip bleeds.

All this way to be together after months apart, and oatmeal instead of a kiss.

Two Flavours

Some days start with whiskers. Some mornings, I roll over to find Sheldon's upper lip still hiding beneath mustache, his eyebrows sending out feelers to my fingertip. His grey eyes. His amused cheek. Often, I rouse to a belt buckle's clink and the jangle of keys dangling from a carabiner on his belt loop. I smell coffee and shoe-shine as he spiffs his steel-toes for work. Some afternoons, our companionship shifts as lips give way to tongues, and words to sounds of pleasure. My body welcomes his body in, and we vanish into trust. Emerge, laughing.

Other mornings, Laura's salty juice jolts me awake instead of coffee. Or I wake with my finger sheathed in her, dowsing essence, and her pleasure is my alarm. Other times, I find the crushed petals of her lips clinging to my hip and her impossible silk spinning down, capturing the pillow.

Some nights, my heart pounds me awake. I hear the voice of the Gay and Lesbian Association's help line attendant replaying in my head: "You're probably a lesbian, afraid to come out." To drown it out, I chant the names of men who made me wet just by standing close to me, and men who broke my heart. I even review my list of childhood crushes.

Night after night, I consider leaving Sheldon. Not because I want to. Because people act like I'm supposed to. The thought of losing him stabs me. I will learn to clutch that pain as an amulet against biphobia. I will stab myself like that at least once a night, for months before I understand.

Years Ago, It Was Dickie Dee

After a breakfast of cold chicken, French bread and berries on the beach, Laura kneeled to kiss my feet. Her long auburn hair threaded between my toes. Later, she washed the sand from her mouth with twenty-five-cent lemonade from a makeshift stand.

Now, motorcycle jackets and bathing suits shucked, I am in her arms in the entryway of her house. Our breasts slide together like oysters. I am here but also I am elsewhere. Divided. Between her and my departure. Between my need to see Sheldon and my need to paint her onto my skin before driving home.

She says, "Do you hear that?"

The ice cream truck!

And suddenly she is out of my arms and out the front door, calling me to follow her down the front walk into the moment, this very moment.

When I do, she puts cold sweetness in my hand. I lick slowly.

SECONDI E CONTORNI

Extreme Hospitality

Sunlight transforms Lake Louise into a luminous reservoir of turquoise ink. A few Japanese tourists bow toward me, smile and go back to taking photos. The shoreline path offers early August's bounty; the first mushrooms and wild strawberries, Alberta wild rose, grass-of-Parnassus and death camas. At the far end of the lake, Victoria glacier's grey run-off swirls into the opaque water, transforming the surface into a sheet of marbled paper. Here, where the Plain-of-Six-Glaciers trail begins at the edge of an alluvial fan, I settle into the solitude as though in the company of an old friend.

Five kilometres and twelve hundred feet of elevation lie between me and my job at the Plain-of-Six-Glaciers teahouse. As the trail gets steeper and emerges from the trees, the sun adds heat to my exertion. The groundwater here may contain giardia cysts, causing "beaver fever," so the trickles along the path seem to tease me about forgetting my water bottle. The teahouse is only about an hour away but my thirst won't wait. My search for wild strawberries becomes a pragmatic one. Catching my breath, I bend to the soil, gently grasp the freckled red berries and tug, careful not to damage the plant. Their glossy skins burst against my tongue, yielding sweet juice.

"Thanks for sharing!" I shout to the bears.

Past the quartzite ledge (mostly dry), and the first gust of glacier-cooled air greets my hot cheeks. My gratitude of nature's "air conditioning" brings forth a deep sigh. Once parallel with the lateral moraine, the signature peaks of this area come into view, forming the lower arc in which the teahouse is nestled. I could be standing inside a painting. To me, the Mitre looks like a sharpened crayon.

Beside it, Mt. Lefroy turns a steep, cold shoulder of grey limestone
to Mt. Victoria, seemingly layered with pristine vanilla icing.

Run-off from the creek streams down the switchbacks. Around
the bend, the teahouse snuggles up against Mt. Whyte. Though
familiarity makes it seem larger, it's the same two-storey stone hut
that's been there for more than seventy years. There's no one on the
top floor's wooden verandah yet. Tibetan prayer flags flutter above
the entranceway.

Inside, Sarah's making a huge pot of soup at the propane prep
stove. Beside her, Rebecca slices still-warm loaves and assembles
four sandwiches at once: hand-mashed hummus, organic cheddar
that I carried up the mountain earlier this week, lettuce from our
alpine *garde-manger*: a cold shed with chicken-wire nailed to the
wooden door to keep the porcupines out. She arranges the sandwiches on deli paper inside baskets, then piles them up to carry past
the wood stove to the dumbwaiter at the corner of the kitchen.

"Where do you want me?" I ask Sarah, eyeing the dishes
piled in three sinks, waiting for hand-washing. Sarah's black hair is
dusted with flour, remnants of bread dough drying on her fingers.
She's already finished the soup and is now rolling out pastry crust
for another apple pie. She was nine months old when her mother
bought the teahouse. Now, she's in her forties and single-handedly
manages the business each season.

"Upstairs. Chris needs help. There must be a lot of Germans
today. We've gone through all five pies already."

"May I take it?" Chris calls down the dumbwaiter shaft,
wanting to know whether it's safe to pull the compartment up to
her level.

"Jus'sec. I'm sending it to you," Rebecca calls up through the
shaft while pushing her glasses up the bridge of her nose with the
back of her index finger. The lenses are spattered with coffee.

Chris's voice is higher-pitched than usual and missing its mischievous lilt. We all know what this means and try to work even faster. Rebecca places the food and pots of tea onto the dumbwaiter's top shelf, then pulls the rope hand-over-hand so that the food rises out of sight. I give my hands a quick wash. A rudimentary system siphons water downhill from an underground spring into the kitchen pipes and a propane heating unit adds the luxury of hot, running water. By the time I dry my hands and stuff the damp paper towel into the wood stove, the dumbwaiter is descending again. Three order sheets lay partially curled on the red-and-white-checkers of its Mac-Tac covering. Rebecca grabs them and starts calling out orders to Sarah. I tie on my apron. I'm too scared to pin on my rainbow flag. I stash it in the bib pocket instead.

"Into the fray!" I say, pushing open the screen door, and hear Sarah yell, "Onward, brave one!" as I climb the steep stairs. The first time I used these stairs, I turned my feet carefully sideways as though climbing a talus slope. Now, I run up them.

It's as busy as I dreaded it would be. Each of the small, red tables has at least two people sitting at it. I shuffle sideways through the narrow space between body parts and the stairway railing. On the way into the serving area, I must squeeze past a family of five clustered around the rectangular table at the front of the verandah. Oblivious to their surroundings, they've piled their gear in the scant space available for manoeuvring among the guests.

Chris is working fast but has it under control, as usual. It humbles me further. She totes up a bill on the adding machine. "Damn. This one's going dead," she says, stabbing at the keys. I yell down the dumb waiter for fresh batteries, our only source of electrical power.

"Table six needs to order, then ten and four." I grab the order pad while she starts to clear the trays of dirty dishes covering the picnic table in front of the hearth. People arrive at the doorway wanting take-out lemonade.

"It's crazy!" I whisper.

"This is nothing," Chris assures me.

But I've never waited tables in my life. For the last ten years, I've been a desk jockey with my own office and people calling me from both ends of the country for advice. I'm twenty years older than the rest of the staff and started two months after they did, right in the middle of the busiest time. I haven't lived apart from Sheldon in a decade. And on top of it all, I must be the only queer on the mountain. Maybe the whole range.

I try to breathe, heading over to table six: the family on summer vacation.

"Hi, folks. What can I get you?" My voice sounds surprisingly bright.

"Howdy," shouts the father. "Do y'all hike up here *every day*?" I've been here only a few weeks but am already tired of this question. Texans feed my growing prejudice, but I manage to answer nicely.

"No. We live up here and hike down for our days off." Anticipating their next question, I add, "I stay in that one," and point over the log railing to the tiny Panabode cabin a stone's throw from the teahouse.

While the kids kick each other under the table, the father proceeds to order practically everything on the menu. His wife debates each of his selections. While they jockey for position as head-of-the-family, another group thumps up the stairway and queues up for a table. I write a few things on the pad but have to cross them out. Finally, I give up and just stand with pen poised above pad, scanning the verandah for signs of revolt at the other tables. Several are waiting to pay and several others haven't yet ordered.

I ask if they need more time, thinking "even though you've already had *at least* twenty minutes!"

Finally, the wife crosses her arms and sits back. "It's too much food. You'll see," she says.

The husband rattles off an endless list and I resist the temptation to quip, "One of everything, then?" In the end, I can't fit it all on the table and they can't fit it all in their stomachs. A lot of it will end up in my backpack the next day: we carry out all the unburnable trash.

Next, table ten. Some kind of blue-blood heiress and her two courtiers. Her look and tone teach me what it's like to be looked upon as "the help."

"This cup is *chipped*," she says. "*And* they are all *cold*. Surely you'll warm them up for us before the tea arrives?" Maybe you should stick them in your armpits! This far out, she's lucky to get hot water without having to haul it herself and start a fire to boil it. I search for something to say that will make her aware of our context.

"I could certainly do that, ma'am, but the wind blowing in from the surrounding glaciers will cool them before they reach the table." I try not to stress the word "glaciers."

Her courtiers come to my rescue. "Oh, never mind. We *are* in the mountains, after all, aren't we?" Identifying their accents as Afrikaans seems to elevate me temporarily above the great unwashed because Her Majesty deigns to tell me she's from Jo-burg. If every customer bugs me, why work here?

Table four. My favourite table. Sitting there, you can't see any other tables, just the view. An older woman sits there alone. She's gazing out over the landscape. Wistfully, it seems to me.

"You okay here? Sorry to keep you waiting."

"No problem. I'm not in a rush. I just scattered my husband's ashes. Up on the moraine. We used to come here every year." I say something sympathetic, trying not to choke up. "Don't worry, love. I'm just fine. Just bring me some Earl Grey, and scones with jam, would you?"

I'm suddenly overwhelmed. Everywhere I look, I see impatient faces. The sheer force of everyone's accumulated need pours into me like bilge into rubber boots. Their need for food, for water, for rest. Their need for *me* to provide it. But how could I ever fulfill it all? Their weariness, hunger and thirst wedges into me, nudging at my nerves. They're hot and cranky and out of breath, out of energy, out of their element. Some look stunned to have made it this far, having just done the biggest hike they have ever or will ever do. It's my job to make them feel safe, fuel them up, and enhance their experience. But instead I want to cry. On my first day I'd washed dishes for five hours straight rather than face all of this *need*.

I should send the orders down on the dumbwaiter. Instead, I run down the steps, plead for a break, and run to the footbridge.

Staring at a flowing stream has always calmed me. The whorls and eddies of water move in many directions at once yet somehow unite in a common current of certain direction and ceaseless abundance. The words of Dylan Thomas make sense to me at last:

The force that drives the water through the rocks
Drives my red blood; that dries the mouthing streams
Turns mine to wax.
And I am dumb to mouth unto my veins
How at the mountain spring the same mouth sucks.

There on the footbridge, tuning into the ongoing rush of my own internal waterways, the incessant creeks and rivers flowing within me, a realization emerges: I go, but don't make myself go. I may go, but the force by which I go is not my own. That force belongs to this realm, the wild realm, and everything I do depends on this ineffable, uncontrollable and boundless energy. And I walk back into the teahouse knowing all needs will be fulfilled, all thirst quenched and hunger sated, but not by *me*. Perhaps *through* me, but not by me.

My first table after my break is in an awkward corner of the wrap-around verandah. So I approach it from inside the teahouse. Two men this time. Crow's feet, laugh lines and flushed faces. I slide open the window next to their table.

"Oh! I didn't realize this was a drive through!" the one with lively eyes and arching eyebrows says, wiping sweat from his neck with a fuschia bandana.

"I'll have a double-double and a maple doughnut," says the other, tucking in his shirt.

"To stay," they say in unison and we all laugh so hard, the other tables look over.

I send their order down on the dumb waiter, then dig into my bib pocket. I'm clumsy with the rainbow pin, but I'm sensing something. ... If they're gay, I want them to feel less alone up here than I do.

This time I squeeze past doffed packs and propped hiking poles to get right beside their table. It's far too busy for striking up conversation but I'm so eager for some queer connection, and curious to find out if my hunch is right.

"We're on our honeymoon," announces the holder of the hanky.

"Yep, finally official after forty years together," says the other groom.

Turns out their first date had been a hike to this teahouse. Same-sex marriage was legalized only last summer.

"At our age, you don't waste time."

✤

After work, I light the candles and place an orange basin beside
the wax-encrusted wine bottles. One litre of hot water carried in a
pitcher from the kitchen is all it takes to get clean. My weekly show-
ers back home have become so decadent: all that water pounding
by the gallon from the showerhead! My cupped hands bring water
to my face. I hear every drop falling back into the basin or onto the
plywood countertop.

Every now and then, a squirrel peeps, or a marmot whistles,
or wind approaches from a distance, sweeping closer and closer
through the sub-alpine fir until it finally buffets the cabin. I welcome
these sounds. They deepen the silence.

I'm dozing on my bunk's luxurious foam when a thunder-
ous rumble begins. It goes on and on, changing in intensity and
frequency, punctuated by *crack!* and *boom!* One of the glaciers is
calving, heaving its burden of rock and snow over the crags, restruc-
turing itself in no uncertain terms. I set my alarm, determined to
hike to the glacier viewpoint before anyone else is on the trail.

I'm impressionable in the morning. It's as though my brain were
clay, pugged by sleep, dampened to a smooth surface by dreams.
Every neural impulse makes a mark: breath entering my nostrils, my
pupils contracting in the light. I feel the planet hugging my bones in
its gravity.

Plain-of-Six Viewpoint is a kilometre beyond the boulder field.
One of the boulders seems to move and a marmot materializes, fur
grizzled with the morning light. She whistles but doesn't leave.

In such a dry, exposed place, unexpected splashes of green
draw me closer to identify the leafy stems tucked beneath jagged
boulders, the lichens finding sustenance on seemingly inhospitable

stone. Cliff woodsia. *Xanthoria elegans* and *Rhizocarpon geographicum.*

My hood keeps the wind out of my ears. It's cold, coming over Lefroy Glacier. Shrubby cinquefoil lines the moist path. I step out of a stand of kruppelholz into the unsheltered stretch of trail. Just then, Upper Victoria Glacier releases a pelting, roaring cascade of snow, ice and rock, pouring down the mountain face and collecting on ledges, settling in flutes on the lower glacier. My breath tumbles out and vanishes, just as I would, were I closer to the source.

When I reach the lateral moraine, the wind increases in speed. A rescue helicopter perched on the moraine last week seemed but a sparrow on a tree branch, and the *whump*-ing of its blades was drowned in the wide-open air above the glacier.

The narrow ridge of jumbled rocks beneath my boots plummets to the grey, cracked surface of Lower Victoria Glacier. One of the crevasses has a boulder wedged inside it, a boulder the size of a semi-trailer.

A gust of wind pushes against me, and I lean into it. Then it dies, leaving me off balance for a moment, as though I'd been resting my weight against a wall that suddenly vanished. Another blast of frigid wind pelts debris into my eyes. What about the ashes? I laugh and laugh, wondering just what I'm wiping from my eyes.

POTS AND PANS

Mom kept kitchen cupboards organized, so organized. A blind person could have found the *mezza luna* for mincing garlic, the *grattugia* for grating cheese.

One day she asked me to fetch the *acciaio inossidabile*. I didn't understand the words so she said, "*Guarda con gli occhi della mente!*" Look with your mind's eye. The only clue she ever gave. She didn't know how to say *stainless steel pot.*

After her funeral, I found the cupboards were full of them.

I'm still cooking in them now. They must be about my age.

CAFFÈ LATTE

I heated the milk in the same pot every morning. Because of its long handle, the little pot would totter slightly on the black coil of the smallest burner until milk weighed it down.

For *caffè latte*, we used instant coffee. The tall jar, square-ish with rounded corners, had a bright red lid. It was a deep lid, almost an inch deep, and textured with grooves. There was no other lid like it in our kitchen. Unscrewing it made a distinctive percussive sound, varying in tone from morning to morning as the jar gradually emptied and the cardboard moisture seal inside the lid turned from clean, glossy white to encircled with fragrant stain.

I always pleaded to be the one to start a new jar. Shiny, gold foil sealed the opening. I loved jabbing a teaspoon through it, hearing the satisfying pop-hiss, inhaling the aromatic burst. A dark brown label wrapped completely around the jar and said "Nescafé" in gold script. One heaping teaspoon of Nescafé would join one of white sugar in an empty mug.

The milk, always 2% Lucerne, had to be heated slowly lest it burn onto the bottom of the pot. If heated too long, however, a skin would form on the milk's surface. If the milk boiled, the skin would re-form as the cup cooled. This I would gather up with the edge of my spoon, mouth contorted in disgust, and relegate to the opposite lip of the mug where it would cling, threatening to slide back in while I squeezed my eyes shut and drank as quickly as possible.

Sometimes this skin would take me by surprise. I'd happily slurp the hot liquid only to feel sludge enter my mouth along with elixir, and I'd have to force myself to let it slide down my throat. It was like swallowing someone else's phlegm.

I learned to use a small strainer to ensure no scum in my lattes. If Mom caught me straining, she'd scold me. It's the best part of the milk, she'd say, the most nutritious. She'd insist I stir it back into the milk and ingest it. Then, while I gulped my *latte* down and scalded myself in the process, she'd reminisce about the fresh milk of her youth, still warm from the cow with thick cream floating on top. It didn't help my gag reflex.

In order to avoid this scalding and scolding, I took to hovering over the little pot of milk, waiting for signs of steam. As soon as it rose in constant wisps from the surface, I'd snatch the pot off the stove and pour the milk onto the brown and white granules waiting at the bottom of the mug. I'd give it a stir while making my way to the table.

Unlike supper, which was religiously eaten together, we'd have breakfast in shifts, based on our own schedules. Our kitchen table was solid wood, the same colour as the *marons glacés* my aunt would sometimes send from Italy. The scent of lemon Pledge lingered. Small dents and scratches etched its polished surface. A trace of writing, illegible but unmistakably cursive, adorned one side. One of us must have pressed too hard on a pen while writing one of the enforced thank you letters to relatives.

For breakfast, we folded the tablecloth in half and draped it over one end of the table. It was sparsely set with a few plates, white sugar, unsalted butter, jam and white bread. My parents never bought brown bread: it was what you ate in wartime when you couldn't afford refined flour. I didn't eat whole wheat until my diet-obsessed teenaged sister started bringing it home. Whole wheat or not, I was still young enough to give my bread a thick layer of butter and not hesitate to sprinkle white sugar on top.

Mom was forever admonishing my teenaged brother and sister not to leave their half-finished *caffè lattes* around the house. Once, upon finding such a mug, Mom carried it down the first flight of stairs in our split-level. Sensing drama about to unfold, I followed. She stopped at the top of the second flight leading to my siblings' rooms on the lower level. I hid where I could see without being seen. My sister was hovering near her doorway while my brother stood against a blank wall, looking up at Mom while she brandished the half-empty ceramic mug. She started yelling. "Whose cup is this? How many times do I have to tell you ..." Whatever the response was, it must have pushed her over the edge because she hurled the cup. At my brother's head. He ducked, just in time, and the cup smashed against the wall. Cold *caffè latte* dripped down onto the orange and brown carpet. I was puzzled for a long time. How could an abandoned mug be such a big deal? It took me years to understand that sometimes a cup is not just a cup.

After Mom died, I switched to skim milk. When my future stepmother came from Italy to marry Dad, she brought a special pot for heating milk. It was enamelled and made of a thick, glazed crockery. Though the milk was less likely to burn or boil in such a pot, it heated too slowly. Anyway, by then we had a microwave. I was always in a hurry to drive across town for university, so I nuked my milk directly in the mug.

After I left home, I couldn't afford Nescafé so it was Maxwell House or Taster's Choice. In my late twenties, when I developed caffeine intolerance, the instant coffee became decaf and the red lid became the glossy green of late summer's poplar leaves. By my early thirties, coffee was too astringent for my reflux-plagued digestion, so the brown granules became barley and chicory from a Caf-Lib jar with a yellow lid. In my health store phase, I sprang for the fancier Bambu, which included powdered figs and acorn and came in a foil-lined cardboard jar with a pull-top seal and plastic press-on lid. I even had to switch from skim milk to soy in the interest of asthma management.

Bambu with soy is about as Italian as shelaileighs. Heated soy with ginger drink powder from Chinatown is delicious on a winter morning but barely connected to my past. I even stopped drinking my *caffè latte* substitutes for a while, so unsatisfying were they. Of course, there were the decaf soy lattes made by baristas along the way, but they never tasted the same as the drink I grew up with.

Finally, in my forties, I happened upon Red Espresso, a finely ground rooibos tea. I blend it with fine-cut cinnamon and steep it in a coffee press, then add honey and soy milk. The colour is satisfyingly coffee-like and the flavour divine. It contains neither milk nor coffee, yet it's the closest thing so far to my childhood *caffè latte*. Better, perhaps: it's good for my body and free of troubling memories. I sit cross-legged, open a notebook in my lap and drink my elixir while writing my first pages of the day with a pen, just as I did in my first diary thirty-nine years ago.

I still have that little stainless steel pot, though I rarely use it. The screw holding it together is rusty but secure. The greying matte handle feels as wise as weathered bone and light as driftwood in my grasp.

Fermenti Lattici

My parents rented a villa for our biannual seaside summer vacation near the Adriatic Sea.

My earliest memory of it is of twirling in the front garden, cotton fabric billowing, orange and red pattern blurring with my turning. The pattern of flowers on my hand-sewn character skirt. The skirt held together at the back with white Velcro rectangles so it could be donned in a dash during dance class and doffed with a rip before softball practice. Twirling in that skirt, I would conjure my black character shoes, the thin strap spanning my instep to hold a glossy button in its eye. In dance class, in this skirt and these shoes, I felt the slow music's minor key tugging me to the ground, and my knees bend – how my hands plunged into earth and my wrists turned, how much work it was to pull up potatoes!

Everyone came to the villa. Mom's family came to stay with us, and Dad's mother. Dad's siblings had summer pied-à-terres a few blocks away and would come for *pranzo*, the largest meal, taken at midday, usually followed by a *pisolino* or nap.

Through the curly patterns and chalky blue paint of the villa's ornate iron fence, I would watch relatives arrive. When they closed the gate, the catch of the latch struck sound from the iron, making the whole fence into a percussion instrument from my parents' *Viva Cugat!* album.

My dad's sister would pedal her *Graziella* to our villa, going the wrong way down the one-way street in a caution-yellow dress, the brim of her floppy sun-hat catching a breeze and flattening over one eye. I remember my grandmother raising her arm during *pranzo*, how she strummed the strings of her fine armpit hair and sang a few lines of "Guantanamera." I remember her denture flopping free around a mouthful, how she dubbed herself *La Nonna al Dente Volante*, Grandmother of the Flying Tooth. I remember Mom's sister placing her fingertips against my belly and jiggling it up and down to ease my indigestion.

In the evenings, teenagers would arrive to pick up my brother and sister. Girls with ample, silky hair. Boys whose woollen sweaters wafted cologne, doubling girls on their Vespas. Girls like the figureheads on the prow of a ship, breasts thrust forward from having their arms behind their backs to hold onto the seat. Boys on idling motorini, tanned legs and leather sandals anchoring their modern-day corsairs. Together, they formed my siblings' *comitiva*. Watching the revving convoy head toward the harbour for a late night of dancing, I would make a wish to grow up very, very fast.

Very early one morning, my brother and sister stumbled into the bedroom, waking me. By the time my feet reached the cool tile floor, they were both already dead asleep.

The bathroom smelled awful. I turned on the light. Red chunks studding the orangey fluid in the bidet looked suspiciously like roma tomatoes. The whole thing was garnished with dark green flakes. The ejected meal, I deduced, had had its origins in *linguine* in a tomato basil sauce.

They must have been at a *spaghettata*. Often after a night of dancing and drinking, friends would head to someone's home for a late-night feed of starchy comfort food. A simple plate of spaghetti is easy enough, even for a drunk cook, and can cheaply feed an entire owl-eyed *comitiva*.

I held my nose and sat on the toilet next to the bidet. I turned the tap on the bidet with my free hand but the large chunks proved to be too much for the small drain to swallow. I went to bed wondering which of them had been sick.

In the morning, they both complained of nausea, headache and thirst. "*Poverini*," Mom said, convinced they had the flu, poor things. And there was only one thing for the flu: *fermenti lattici*.

The glass ampoules filled with pale yellow liquid lay cushioned in a box. Their shape echoed a long, wrapped candy: wide and rounded in the middle and tapering suddenly to narrower ends. I'd never seen anything like them in Canada. When I was sick, I expected small pills, nasal sprays, saline drops and cherry-flavoured syrups. At home, the most medically unpleasant thing we endured was a rectal thermometer. But these *fermenti* seemed downright medieval. Where had she found them? There was even a little saw in the box.

Mom showed us how to safely remove one end of the ampoule. Thus decapitated, it resembled a miniature champagne flute with a pointy stem, although the pale yellow liquid tasted nothing like the Asti Spumante we had every Christmas.

She made us drink the *fermenti* straight up. I say "us" because the flu is contagious so, naturally, Mom assumed I'd catch it, too. Better to make a pre-emptive strike. She was nothing if not proactive. "Go on. It's good for you," she said. *Dai, fa bene*!

We were quaffing a concoction of lactobacillus strains used for making yoghurt. Imagine unsweetened, unflavoured yoghurt. Super-concentrated but liquidy, the consistency of saliva. And add a twist of lime. Something you could confidently rely on to induce vomiting. My siblings tossed their first ones down like evil shooters then locked eyes, willing each other not to gag.

A single dose was not enough, no. One had to take an ampoule daily. For a week. When we found that out, my sister and brother exchanged exaggerated looks and hidden gestures. I soon understood these as silent micro-arguments in which they settled the issue of whether to confess to being hungover. They never did.

I missed out on the Vespas, the dancing, the crushes and the *spaghettata*. I couldn't reminisce with them later about that epic party. But I could write myself into their memories of the aftermath.

So, when my brother and sister marched into the kitchen every morning, I marched with them. Together, we would line up at the counter to saw open our vials of ick. Meanwhile, Mom would wash the thermometer. She'd shake the mercury down and puzzle at their lack of fever, while I monitored my own forehead with the inside of my wrist and faked a cough.

REMEDIES

On summer evenings in Grado, my family would go for a *passeggiata* along the waterfront.

A *passeggiata* is more than a stroll. In order to qualify as a *passeggiata*, your steps must be slower than your heartbeat. Over time, your footfalls create a syncopy or an echo of your pulse. My mother called this rhythm *caplin-caplòn*.

In a *passeggiata*, there may be a sweater draped over your shoulders, sleeves hanging or loosely tied over the chest. There's an arm through yours, the arm of someone you care about, and you gently rest your free hand on the forearm or bicep of this person, creating a loop of affection. Or perhaps your hand surrounds the sticky hand of a child, or your fingers entwine loosely in those of your lover. And you're surrounded by many others doing the same, everyone synchronized to the rhythm of *caplin-caplòn*, and headed not nowhere exactly but *chissà?* who knows where, wherever you happen to go.

The *passeggiata* was always accompanied by *gelato*. I can still see our favourite *gelateria* glowing incandescent in the humid summer night, and the grinning man in a white jacket behind the counter. My uncle would fold my hand around a coin. I'd run over the cobblestones. Nearing the counter, I would see how his jacket strained at the buttons across his belly.

Night after night, I placed the same order from a tippy-toed stance while trying not to drool: *Coppa del Nonno*. The *gelataio* would hand me a brown plastic cup about the size of a cappuccino and a paper-wrapped wooden "spoon." It was more like a paddle, about the size and width of Mom's thumb, and it narrowed in the middle slightly, like an hourglass or infinity symbol. I'd pull open the lid by its little tab. The underside of the white, waxy disc was always coated with coffee *gelato* and I always started by licking it clean.

A *coppa* is more than a cup. It's also a prize, and that coffee ice cream was certainly a prize for me — on the surface. Yet a *coppa* is also a grail; a hollow or empty area; a destiny or a predetermined course, as in "take this cup away from me"; and a potion or a remedy. I would come to know all of these meanings.

The persistent presence of a *Coppa del Nonno* on those *passeggiate* now strikes me as profoundly ironic. The words mean Grandfather's Cup, but the only grandfather ever on that *passeggiata* was the cup cradled in my little hand. My father's father had died while my mother was still pregnant with me. My mother's father had disappeared when she and her sister were children. That was all she'd ever said about him. But I've since learned it hadn't been that simple.

In 2010, I ended a twenty-three-year absence with a visit to my mother's sister in Italy. Zia began by telling me my nonna, a Northerner, had married a Sicilian, and he hadn't simply disappeared. He'd abandoned his family outright. He was a gambler who beat his pregnant wife with a belt when she failed to help him on with his coat. He'd left home as a teenager and only came back to drop off his two small daughters at his mother's and then disappear. When Mom's older sister was born, their mother was alone and had nothing. She relied on neighbours for food during her confinement. Nonna had once polished off seven bowls of minestrone in one sitting following a period of starvation.

Nonna married young. In Zia's view, her mother had been stuck, arrested in her development, her maturity. She'd never quite seized the full reality of motherhood, the concomitant responsibilities. Nor had she ever felt the emotions that are supposed to come naturally to a mother.

My mother had described her mother to me as a single mother, a travelling saleswoman who had found the safest place for her daughters to wait out the war: a convent in the foothills of the Alps. Since the war lasted about six years, I had thought that had been the length of their stay. Actually, their mother left them with the nuns when my mother was four years old, and she'd stayed there until she was fourteen. My mother spent all of her formative years in that convent. Her stories of mistreatment at the hands of the nuns suddenly seemed that much more horrifying.

I also understood something my stay-at-home mom had said when I was about sixteen. Since my siblings had left home and I was mostly grown up, I wondered why she didn't get a part-time job or volunteer somewhere. At first, she said her English wasn't good enough. When I pressed the subject, she finally said, "I vowed that when I had children, I would always be at home for them."

How did my mother manage to mother me when she'd never been mothered herself?

My *zia* used to recriminate their mother for not loving them, and her father for leaving them. Now she forgives them.

"They were so innocent. At eighteeen, my mother was still using her slipper as a cradle for her rag doll, for God's sake."

After hearing this adult version of my maternal history, I went up the elevator to Nonna's old bed-sit. Sitting on the mattress Nonna had slept on for years, I slowly absorbed the fact that my mother had essentially been abandoned by both of her parents.

I know how to love because I was loved as a child. But how did my mother know?

My mother referred to the convent as an *asilo*. I used to think it meant kindergarten. Now I know it also means a refuge or shelter for those in need. It could also mean orphanage.

I grew up with Laura Ingalls, not Anne Shirley. I used to

wonder why my mother hadn't given me *Anne of Green Gables*, a Canadian classic, instead of *Little House on the Prairie*. Unfamiliar with children's books in English, she would have relied on the recommendations of bookstore staff. Anne seems the obvious choice. Anne was so much more like me. Loquacious, imaginative and an aspiring writer.

Now I think maybe the bookstore clerk had indeed recommended Anne, but her orphan tale was too close to my mother's own story, a story she wanted to protect me from. Instead, she wanted me to fall asleep on the banks of Plum Creek and dream about a simple house warmed by a family idyl she'd never had. The family idyl she'd wanted to create for me.

I finally met Anne of Green Gables as an adult. I cried then, and I still do every time I read that book. At first, I was mystified by my intense empathy for this orphan. After all, I had a father, a sister and a brother. I'd had a mother. I knew how it felt to be loved and cherished, to be cradled within the belonging of a family.

Eventually, I came to acknowledge my inner Anne. In the wake of the undertaker's hearse, our family unmoored and we sailed apart, hawsers trailing. For me, Mom had been an immovable, reliable pier. But a human mother can never be more than an anchor buoy, impermanent and vulnerable to squalls.

Cancer forced my mom to leave me. What happened with my dad? After my decision to leave home — sooner than he deemed appropriate and for reasons he didn't comprehend — I went decades without feeling he loved me. He never sought me out and when I called him, our talks were awkward and short. I can only speculate as to why. It was as though I'd been dropped off on the front stoop of adulthood and never picked up again.

Abandonment is a pernicious form of absence. Through the lens of family history, I discern its contours lurking within each generation. I've come to view my fear of abandonment as an ancestral wound, handed down to me as part of a complex family history. From that vantage point, my childhood *Coppa del Nonno* seems a kind of pre-emptive potion, a remedy for an emptiness I had yet to experience.

These days, when the old wound begins to ache, I take a walk. I remember that seaside *passeggiata* and how close we all were before my mother died. How she, the orphan, was both harbour and anchor for all our boats. And before long, I'm synchronized to the rhythm of *caplin-caplòn*, headed not nowhere exactly but *chissà?* who knows where, wherever I happen to go.

THE CODE

A Ziploc bag full of pepperoni sticks was dangling from my teeth
when Tasha said she loved me. Said it first, and unexpectedly. She
stood there, dangling and exposed while I held a baguette between
my knees and re-shouldered my backpack and re-clipped the hip
strap. Likely she was squinting at me in the sunshine, but I wouldn't
know. I was staring at my hiking boots in the spring snow. The life-
line-like creases. The dark of wet leather. The nicks in the rands.

I finally said, "Wow! Cool." And that was all.

It was the first time that a woman – a woman that I *wanted* –
had said, "I love you."

And for the first time, I wasn't the first one to say it. And for
the first time, my feelings were being reciprocated.

We were fresh from the canyon, the raven's nest, the chick's
wide gullet, the nude raspberry branches offering thorns, and the
lichen, thriving. Was it before we made our detour into the bush,
seeking sunshine on bare skin? Before we rocked each other beside
the rocks?

When that mourning cloak fluttered by on the way to lay its
eggs, the snakes had already moulted. We had found their shed
skins in the sulphur springs. They will change skins again and again
before they're through with the vapours of the marsh, the perennial
watercress, the moss and stone.

The snake and the butterfly whisper, "Grow!" They are beyond
me. I am forty. A woman has – at last! – said these words to me and
here I sit, still ruminating about transformation while serpents have
long since abandoned the quasi-transparent tubes of who they once
were, and caterpillars are already enjoying their bird's-eye view.

"A woman loves me!" I was thinking as we walked along. Not my sister or my mother, not my aunt or my cousin. Not my best friend. But a woman whose lips and fingers and tongue and nipples and thighs and pussy tune to my own like the striking of a mutual fork, flesh oscillating at a pitch audible through walls and pillows and palms. That kind of a woman loves me!

It has taken me days to absorb it, to welcome it. It has taken days for those words to slip through the joints of fear's carapace and begin to stroke my heart with a most divine effleurage.

A woman said, "I love you!" and I didn't say it back. I was close but my heart's voice was inaudible above the clanging alarm.

I've learned how to keep loving Sheldon even when my heart is broken. But I still don't know how to let two people's love in at once. No one's ever stuck around long enough for me to learn. The level of vulnerability is breathtaking. How does anyone handle it?

Yet this is what I've wanted for so long. My heart broke and broke again for wanting this. Eventually, I stopped hoping. I clung to my belief that it was possible.

So I guess "Wow! Cool" are the right words, aren't they?

The other words? Give me time. It hasn't gone well for me with these words and women. The very first time I ever told a woman I loved her, I had a panic attack while I waited for her to say something. And when I had recovered, she said, "I love you. I'm not in love with you."

The second time I said it was to a woman who was leaving me. She was wearing a white wife-beater, stained. I was pulling petals off a daisy and throwing them at her and realizing she was ugly to me for the first time. I said the words, not as an incantation to make her stay, only so she would know what miracle she was wasting.

The three little words are not magic words. They're more like a mantra gradually shaping each day into the swirling current of a life together. Not a presto, but a metamorphosis.

Now here I am, three days later, saying it back. I am on my knees in front of her. My face is wet. She is on my armchair. Her dark velvet thighs against the yellow throw are trembling slightly, like pollen on the stamen of a lily.

She may have heard "I love you" before, but my meaning of the words is this: "My being responds with emotions and sensations only possible with a certain depth of feeling, with a certain fitting together of hearts. I feel safe with you. When I'm with you, time ceases to pass. When I'm with you, I am happy. When I'm with you, it's as though I were dreaming."

My three little words are a code. When cracked, they read, "I am prepared to be transformed."

DA PEPPE

"*Vieni*," says Peppe, and I follow him down the cellar stairs. His white deli smock glows in the faint light from beyond the open door. Keeping my eyes fixed to the beacon of his broad back, I feel for each step with my toe, thrilled to be going where other customers are not allowed.

Dad wants to buy the freshest product in the store, so here I am, standing in the dark. As my eyes adjust, I find a barrel next to me, so big I could stand up inside it. Peppe dips a long-handled skimmer down into its hidden contents. The liquid dripping from the skimmer back into the barrel echoes eerily, as if the cellar's invisible walls were leaking.

I try not to think of Poe, how his Fortunato was lured by a cask of amontillado into a niche of Montressor's cellar only to be slowly interred behind a growing wall of bricks. I focus instead on my belly.

I'm still a bit carsick from Dad's driving. The slipped disc in his back prevents him from keeping constant, even pressure on the gas. His passengers must endure the nauseating sensation of acceleration and deceleration as he alternately presses and eases off the pedal. I had to endure it all the way from home in the southeast to Peppe's store in the northeast of the city.

The night before, Dad had driven us to Italian school after supper. We'd had *fegato*, liver, which I hated but Mom had a five-strip policy. I had to eat that much before she'd let me leave the table. This time, I surreptitiously dropped the strips into the paper napkin in my lap, then stuffed it into my bookbag, handmade by Mom from an old pair of jeans. I could smell the organ meat every second of the cross-town journey in that rocking car. I barely made it to St. Alfonsus without vomiting. As soon as we got there, I threw the fetid bundle in the garbage. It was one of the only times I ever managed to get away with anything.

But when my dad said, "*Andiamo da Peppe*," I happily went along. A little carsickness was worth it for the fizzy *chinotto* I would get to drink while dad shopped for groceries not available at Safeway.

I would sit at the deli counter, savouring my bittersweet pop, while Dad chatted with Peppe. I would tune out the content of their conversation and listen instead to the music of Peppe's *meridionale* accent, so different from my parents' northern inflections.

Peppe would switch on the electric meat slicer. The shiny metal hummed as it worked. With his arm as big around as a log of bologna, he propelled the blade through cured flesh with precision and ease. His right hand set a perfect rhythm – push forward pull back, push forward pull back – as his left hand syncopating, moving right to left between the machine and the counter, while his fingers, fat as *cotechino* sausages, caught and delicately draped the meat slice-over-slice onto a glossy square of brown butcher paper. His motions were like a deconstructed Sign of the Cross, blessing scrumptious food.

Peppe always gave Dad a sample of the coldcuts he was buying. Dad relished this simple generosity of freshly sliced meat tucked inside a small bun with a thin crust and plenty of white crumb. I ate these every day myself for lunch at school. My favoured *mortadella*, with its Smartie-sized discs of white fat and bisected peppercorns scattered throughout the thin, pink flesh, was a far cry from the "baloney" my classmates ate. Their neat, identical sandwiches smeared with condiments mystified me. Their pink squares of lunch meat riddled with pieces of macaroni and blobs of cheese made me grimace.

My *panino* held a new delight every day. *Prosciutto crudo.*
Capocollo. Pancetta. I'd help my dad re-wrap these meats at home,
while he imitated Peppe's accent and gestures. He was really good
at it and usually had all of us in stitches with pretending he was
meridionale.

Dad showed me how to transfer the meat without touching it
with my fingers. He'd unfold the paper, slide a palm under it and,
turning his wrist smoothly, pat the meat down on a length of plastic
wrap, then peel away the paper. He showed me how to smooth the
Saran Wrap over the meat so as not to trap any air inside, and seal
the wrap to itself so no air could get at the food. Inside the fridge, the
neat, crisp packages reminded me of a stack of typewriter paper.

Peppe had smelly feet. I mean really stinky, as though hanging
around that deli case for years had infused him with the stench of
Gorgonzola and Stilton combined.

Sometimes, he came to visit us. He'd take off his coat and
shoes in the entryway between the two flights of stairs in our split
level. The warm, leather loafers would lie like wet dogs on the rug,
practically steaming with odour. You could almost see wavy vertical
lines emanating upwards, like something from a comic book. He
would cross his black business-socked feet at the ankles and rest
them on the amber-coloured hardwood floor.

While he and my dad visited in the upstairs living room, my
sister and I made a game of creeping up the stairs, sniffing carefully at each step to determine at which point we could detect his
rank bouquet. Once we caught a whiff, we'd rush back down into
the basement gripping our throats and pinching our noses. We'd
press my sister's bedroom door shut and exhale in gusts accompanied by sounds of strangulation and gagging, then roll around
feigning loss of consciousness. And then we'd do it again.

❧

I draw my finger down the row of *p* s. "Payne, Peters, Peugeot ... Peppe's, Peppe's ... why isn't it listed?"

I'm almost thirty years old before a craving for *torrone* propels me to the White Pages. I want to make a special trip to stock up on my childhood favourites. Surely I can find the place by memory, I tell myself.

As it turns out, I'm wrong about that. I cruise up and down Centre Street so many times I begin to feel like a junkie waiting for her hookup. I even look in my rear view mirror, expecting to see flashing red-and-blues. Eventually, I stop to call my sister from a pay phone for directions.

When I finally pull into the parking lot, I'm momentarily confused. Though the marquee says Italian Supermarket, the storefront looks just like Peppe's. Finally, it dawns on me: the place was never officially called Peppe's.

These days, Peppe's has a small café up front, near the cash registers. A free-standing stone oven has been added, too. It looks like a giant Mexican *chimenea* was lowered in through the roof. The man making pizza looks like a miniature Pillsbury Doughboy in front of the oven. The fire, well banked and cloaked in ash, is as comforting and homey as a grey cashmere sweater.

I start browsing the housewares, expecting the familar tablecloth patterns, olive oil decanters and *formaggiere* to provoke an emotional reaction. The selection is limited and I don't feel much at all. On to the canned beans. *Lupini, borlotti, lenticchie.* Still nothing. At my back lies an oasis of freshly baked breads. *Ciabatte, schiacciate, foccacie, panini.* They shimmer with delicious scent but they might as well be a mirage in the desert of my gluten intolerance. I'm unmoved by my beloved cheeses, phlegmatic over *mascarpone*, stoic before *asiago* and apathetic about *fontina*.

On to the olives — olives and more olives, aligned in rows of clear plastic troughs with stainless steel pierced spoons poised amidst them. Compared to the cellar olives of that childhood visit, these ones are so blatant and diverse. Glossy, green ones with tongue-like garlic cloves protruding slightly from their middles. Smooth, ovoid black ones that would fit to my palate like miniature eggs. Smaller oily ones, wrinkled all over like raisins. Which type had Peppe been scooping up for us back then? In my recollection, only one type existed, a quintessential olive trickling with the mystery of the unseen. These olives dredged up and arrayed in the light of day unsettle me.

I find myself inhibited about approaching the deli case. Ever since I pulled open the shop door I've been imagining myself striding up to the besmocked staff and confidently ordering *due etti di mortadella*. Now, a sudden and uncharacteristic shyness grips me.

Three women and a man stand behind the case. None of them resemble Peppe. Could that short, young man be Peppe's son? Or would it be his grandson by now?

My peculiar reticence makes me dodge into the pasta aisle. I scan the varieties while working up my nerve. *Fusilli.* For some reason, I am reluctant to speak Italian here. *Rotelle.* In Italy, I have no such compunction. What, exactly, is the issue? *Pappardelle, tagliatelle, fettuccine.* Haven't I been told time and again that my Italian is excellent? Look at those *orecchiette.* Didn't I translate a novella by Italo Calvino? *Farfalle* and *conchiglie.* Am I ... intimidated? No way. *Orzo.* I'll just go up there and speak Italian, already.

I approach the deli case. Only one person behind it seems even remotely Italian — and not just because he's loafing while his female colleagues scurry about. He's short and a little swarthy. I stare vacantly at the *soppressata.* Finally, the red-haired woman asks if she can help me. I take a deep breath.

"*Sono curiosa. Quanto costerebbe una ruota intera di par-miggiano? Reggiano.*"

The short man smirks. It doesn't occur to me that he finds my notion of buying a whole wheel of parmesan amusing. Instead, I'm certain he takes me for a WASP who's picked up some badly-accented Italian.

"I'm writing some memories of being here as a child," I say, hoping to legitimize myself.

While he looks me over and says nothing, the red-haired woman replies in a Polish-accented English, "That would be a lot of cheese. About forty or fifty kilos."

She points to two rounds of cheese stacked on top of the deli case. One of them rests against the other at an angle, like tires in the midst of being changed. Each wheel is as deep as half a wine cask. Block letters spell out Parmiggiano Reggiano around the circumference. The words are melted right into the rind, like one of my childhood wood-burning projects.

"That's strange. I have a memory of my aunt giving me a full wheel of *parmiggiano* once. It was only about this big." I use my hands to illustrate, cupping my palms around an invisible wheel of parmesan.

"That," she says, pointing at the car tires, "is how they are exported."

"Ah. So maybe the small wheels are only available in Italy. But I'm curious. How much would one of those big ones cost?"

"About fifteen hundred, maybe."

Not so bad. Slightly cheaper than a semester of tuition for my master's degree.

She shows me parmesan in sealed packages, back at the case I'd previously disregarded in my quest for the whole cheese. One piece weighs three hundred grams and costs eleven dollars and seventy-seven cents. She's underestimated the cost of that spare tire. At thirty-eight dollars and ninety-nine cents per kilo, a wheel would actually cost just under two thousand dollars. I think I'll finish my degree.

The prepackaged triangles are disappointing and somehow impersonal, more Safeway than Peppe. I'd imagined getting some cut to order by a person, an Italian who might pinch my cheeks and hand me a *panino*. I buy a piece of shrink-wrapped Reggiano anyway.

I wander past the espresso-ground coffees, recognizing the Medaglia d'Oro, the Caffè Mauro, the Lavazza from my loved ones' cupboards. Next, the herbal teas. A box of chamomile stops me dead. No matter what was wrong with me, my mom would steep *camomilla* and add honey and lemon. Along with Nivea cream, chamomile tea was her panacea. I stare at this box of Bonomelli, her preferred brand. Its cheery, yellow block letters stand out just as I remember them, against a background of cobalt blue. Chamomile flowers still blossom from a white cup against a sky-blue background. My favourite colours as a child, all here on one box of tea. I wonder if that's a coincidence.

Any of the customers waiting at the checkout line could be northern Italian, like me, including the strawberry blonde and the redhead. But they could also be Irish, or Czech. I look like any of the other lovers of Italian food who roam these aisles. But I have a history here, I want to tell them. Peppe himself sliced my *mortadella*.

At the cash register, I make one last attempt to connect. The cashier is a teenager but I think I see some *meridionale* traits in his dark eyes and dark hair.

"Are you related to the owners?" I ask the cashier, but no, he just works there part-time.

"The owner's right there," he says, pointing to a man in the café.

He looks portly and middle-aged. He's wearing a baseball cap bearing the Italian flag, leaning forward on his elbows and talking to another man across the small table. His gaze flicks up at me for a second when he feels me looking at him. He has bags under his eyes. Maybe *he* is the elusive Son of Peppe? Maybe I should go and introduce myself? I catch myself sniffing for a lingering scent of blue cheese and hide my smile.

I treat the walk to my car like a *passeggiata*. Grocery bags swing gently from my hands. I try to convince myself to go back inside and talk to the owner. I fail.

Several men are unloading a shipment of large pails into the dock. I watch them, hoping they will see me and wonder why I'm lingering beside my vehicle. Maybe one of them will strike up a conversation. He'll be Peppe's nephew or cousin and we will reminisce together.

I linger beside my car and drink an entire can of cold *chinotto* before finally admitting it: I want to feel I belong here. And yet, somehow, I just can't let myself. Why?

This question marinates in my consciousness for days afterward before the answer emerges. To feel connection, that sweet effervescence, I must reconcile the girl daunted by dark cellars with the woman who dares to create a life from scratch, who freed herself through acts of self-invention. How? And if I succeed, will all my progress be splintered by history's unyielding pit?

So many neglected memories, lurking in the dark by the barrelful. Unbidden, my mind at last plunges into invisible reservoirs. Like Peppe's long-handled skimmer, it surfaces laden with cured fruit.

PARMIGGIANO

When Mom calls me from the kitchen, she cycles through the first syllable of my siblings' names before happening upon the right combination of sounds.

There she stands, at one arm of the U-shaped kitchen, stirring a pot on the stove. A neat bow of apron strings lies against the patterned cotton of her housedress. She's making *ragú* for tonight's pasta. Soon, my dad will get home from work and we'll all sit down for supper.

She asks me to check if there's enough grated *parmiggiano* for supper. I take the *formaggiera* out of the fridge and flip open its stainless steel lid. The scalloped bowl of the spoon lies among a few crumbs of cheese. The fluted glass dish is nearly empty. So I take my place at the other arm of the kitchen's U, my back only an arm's reach away from Mom's, and begin the ritual.

Slide wooden cutting board out of slot in countertop. Unwrap *parmiggiano* wedge. Get grater out of drawer. Unfold hinged arm. Prop *grattuggia* at forty-five degrees within its tray. Push end of grater unit against counter's edge for resistance. Take *parmiggiano* in hand. Rub briskly against tightly packed hexagonal surface as though brushing a honeycomb of teeth.

Once there's enough cheese in the tray, I hold the *parmiggiano* like an apple and bite off a hunk of cheese. When Mom sees the teeth marks, she cuffs the back of my head.

I learn to wait for Mom's back to be turned before I steal a bite. I interrupt my grating ever so briefly to avoid telegraphing my crime. I scrape my front teeth shallowly against the cheese, then quickly grate away the evidence.

Parmiggiano is still one of my favourite cheeses. Newly purchased, it's a triangle with a slightly curved rind of thick *scorza* on which you can discern truncated letters that once marked the outside of the wheel as Parmiggiano Reggiano or Padano. My parents preferred *Reggiano*. When the wedge is partially used, the surface of the cheese arcs slightly, having taken the shape of the grater.

I'm not sure what it cost back then, but now a properly aged *Reggiano* costs about thirty-nine dollars a kilogram. Our fridge was always stocked with a wide variety of cheeses: *provolone, cacciocavallo, parón* and *gorgonzola*. Unlike the rest, *parmiggiano* was not to be eaten in pieces. It could be sprinkled on other foods like pasta or *minestrone*, but that was all.

Savouring a piece just now, I noticed in particular its grainy texture against my teeth. Suddenly it dawned on me that this is why one of the names for parmiggiano is *il grana*, a masculine noun. In the feminine, however, *la grana* refers to the grain or texture of a substance. *Grana* is also slang for trouble and, not surprisingly, it is usually used in the plural, *grane*.

The summer I turned twenty, I was visiting my mother's sister.

Zia's style and carriage evoke the glamour of Sofia Loren. She has Elizabeth Taylor's dramatic arched eyebrows, Marilyn's carefully painted lips, Rita Hayworth's insouciant-yet-poised posture while smoking, and Ingrid Bergman's feminine innocence. She works a fur collar better than women half her age. Whenever I catch the scent of Marlboros, I think of her.

She and my dad hadn't spoken to each other in the years since my mom's death. He'd done something that she took as disrespect to my mother's memory. In the aftermath, it seemed my aunt was trying to get us to take sides. I felt caught in the middle. For that and other reasons, my grieving process became complicated, to the point that it hadn't even begun. Talk about *grane*.

Her birthday present to me that summer was an entire wheel of parmiggiano Reggiano. We were in her modest, modern kitchen. She broke open the wheel and handed me a knife. I inserted the tip of its blade half an inch into the top of the cheese and pried a chunk free. After so many years of furtive bites, having a whole mouthful of *grana* felt like eating gold bullion.

Her husband sat opposite me at the little white table. My uncle smiled. This made his upper lip almost disappear up into his white moustache and his eyes dance like candleflames behind his glasses. And then he chuckled. He had a contained, low-pitched and vibrating laugh, as though mirth were ricocheting around his organs like the ball in a pinball machine. Zio's round belly jiggled visibly beneath his fine silk shirt as I feasted on the "forbidden" cheese.

Both of them just sat back and witnessed my joy. I catch myself watching Sheldon in exactly the same way when he eats corn on the cob.

My mom never wasted anything. She was reducing, re-using and re-cycling before anyone ever thought up the term "environmentalist."

We'd grate the *parmiggiano* right down to the *scorza*, then she'd soak the quarter-inch thick rind. She'd clean it, scraping away the outermost layers. The white rectangle would glide into a pot of minestrone and disappear like a precious gem, seemingly lost forever. There it would simmer, mingling with the vegetables and beans, only to reappear on someone's spoon during supper.

Mouth watering, I'd watch Mom ladle out the *minestrone*, wondering in whose bowl that *scorza* would be, hoping it would be mine. Even after all that soaking and simmering, the *scorza* would still be as chewy as beef jerky and bursting with flavour.

Through many years of silence followed by one or two tearful long-distance phone calls, Zia and I found our way to an understanding. She is the last connection to my maternal line.

After twenty-three years, I finally sit again at her table. Sheldon is at my side, but her love has succumbed to lung cancer. Zia is smoking a different brand. I have forgotten all about the *scorza*, its resilient saltiness. No one but my mother has ever cooked such a thing for me and she's been dead for more than half my lifetime.

On our fifth night together, Zia serves us *minestrone*. And suddenly, there it is, half-hidden in my bowl: *scorza*. My voice catches on an exclamation of surprise. Zia gazes into my tear-filled eyes. In her easy chuckle, I hear the echo of my uncle's laughter. I savour the *scorza* and add my own salt to the bowl.

THE GARDEN

My mind said exercise. Instead, I followed my "wouldn't it be love-ly?" inspiration and took the twenty-minute walk suggested in Julia Cameron's *The Vein of Gold.*

My mind said Bow Falls. Instead, I followed my inner prompting to diverge from the down-river path. I went right instead, pulled open a wrought-iron gate and walked up the flagstones toward Cascade Gardens.

Flowers lined the walk, two by two, unknown by name and colourful. I slowed down. I resisted the other visitors, talked to and acknowledged no one. I looked at geraniums and started to cry.

No. First I noticed poppies up ahead. Small, yellow blossoms floating above slender stalks. Their brazen, crepe-papery openness unlocked a childhood memory of the garden beside our childhood house. One or two oriental poppies guarded the gate, which was more like a section of white fence that swung open and had a black latch of imitation wrought-iron. The poppies were large and bright orange.

It was then my eyes filled with geraniums and tears. And then, as if a magician were pulling a never-ending scarf knot-by-knot out of a top hat, I remembered the peonies. White or ballet-pink blossoms, so heady with layer within layer of soft-as-lips petals that their stems became weak in the knees. Even ants couldn't resist stroking the sweet velvet all over with their feet. I remembered Mom, pruning sheers in one hand, flowers head-down in the other. Mom rustling the silky heads above the lawn, then again in the kitchen sink before arranging them.

I came to some other flowers and their name easily floated to mind. Begonias. My gaze fell into the deep sapphire hearts of small indigo flowers and "lobelia" offered itself. My knowing these flowers surprised me. How long had it been since lobelia arose in my mind? I don't walk by them in others' gardens, or even think about them. A national park has been my home and the wilderness my backyard for almost two decades. Shooting stars, moccasin flowers, glacier lilies and moss campion are what bloom in my world.

Now I felt the source of the mystery. I know these names because of love. Mom said these names, said them over and over because she loved them.

"My mom loved flowers." It's the kind of thing people say about the dearly departed, to remember who they were. Jimmy had a fondness for gin. Gustaf adored outdoor gear. Eulogies are full of these verbal character sketches. It's twenty-eight years since Mom died and this is the first time I think of such a phrase. What do you call a memory stumbled upon as a discovery? There's so much I don't remember about her. But today I know: Mom loved flowers. I dawdled along repeating this mantra.

Giant pea pods bordered the rock stairs, their green bodies split open and spilling white bells. I dropped onto the rundlestone step and leaned my nose in to them. It was a reflex, the action of a marionette directed by invisible strings. Lily-of-the-Valley, *muguets*, *mughetti*. I know three words for them because Mom loved them most of all. The burst of fragrance released a montage, images cascaded from my memory like blooms from a basket: African violets, *bougainvillea*, *oleandri*. Tourists milled around taking photos while I sat on that cold stone as though unhinged, sniffing and sniffing the bouquet. It's something you'd do on the anniversary of someone's death. Remember that side-of-the-house flower bed from thirty-four years ago, the patch of *mughetti* close to the gate. My mom loved flowers.

Nearby, the gardener was talking to some tourists on the burl log bridge. "It's sad because we get everything planted – and it's quite small when we plant as you can see – and then it's pretty much dead-heading throughout July and August. And by September it's mostly over. All that work. And it's over so quickly."

I'm not so sure about that. In the right soil, they can endure for decades.

FRUTTI E FORMAGGI

THE PASTA MACHINE

Our holiday feasts always began with a pasta dish, as is traditional in Italian multi-course meals. The pasta was made by hand at our kitchen table as a family event.

One of us would drape a red-and-white chequered oilcloth over the table. Beneath the red-and-white squares, etched into the wax of the table's polished surface, lay the historical graffiti of family life: partial loops of cursive script, dents, and burn scars of discoloured polish.

Whoever lifted the pasta machine out of its faded box would leave fingerprints on its shiny stainless steel. At one end of the table, we'd line the machine up with the edge and stabilize it with a clamp. A folded cardboard "cushion" prevented the metal from leaving an impression on the wood.

Before long, a mini Vesuvius of white flour would rise from the wooden cutting board beside the machine, its crater brimming with egg and water. These would be blended and kneaded against the board until the dough was as resilient, smooth and pliable as flesh.

Dad would cut off a piece of dough, lay it on a floured area of the cutting board and lean on it with his palm. Then he'd feed it through the machine.

The machine had three slots. The one with rollers was always used first. It produced sashes of pasta used for assembling *lasagne*, *ravioli*, or *tortellini*.

The space between the rollers was controlled by a chrome dial that clicked crisply into place on each setting. Dad worked the dial with a flick of his thumb as though he were winding a watch or the film in his old camera. The flattened dough would go through on the widest setting first. He cranked the handle that turned the rollers that pushed the pasta through to the bottom, where he'd catch it. Then he'd dangle the flat edge of the dough above the rollers, lining it up with the gap, and feed it through again. He'd fold the pasta over, renewing its thickness. Then the rollers pressed it thin again. He did this over and over, as though tempering steel for a sword. Occasionally an air bubble would get pressed out through the layers, making a snapping sound like chewing gum. The lengthening pasta would drape over his thick fingers as it got thinner. Once the pasta had reached the right consistency, he gave it a few finishing passes through the narrowest setting.

If we were making plain pasta, then Dad would feed the thin sash through one of the other slots. Rather than flattening the pasta, these rollers cut it by means of wide or narrow grooves. The wide grooves produced *tagliatelle* – perfect with *burro e parmiggiano*, their wide, flat surfaces slippery with butter and sharp with parmesan cheese. The narrow grooves yielded *capelli d'angelo*, but we rarely used angel hair.

Years later, the manual machine would be replaced with an electric PastaMatic, in which nothing was touched until it was fully formed. Ingredients were combined and kneaded in a sealed chamber. The shape of the PastaMatic output was determined by discs screwed onto the end of an extrusion cylinder. Dad needed only to stand there to sever the pasta into the desired length, gather and arrange and sprinkle it with flour.

I always stared as the pasta extruded from the cylinder, although I found the sight disturbing. It reminded me of the Fuzzy Pumper Barber and Beauty shop by Play-Doh. You, "the barber," would place a ball of Play-Doh inside the client's perforated plastic head and snap her skull closed like a box. Then, by turning a crank, you pressured the contents of your client's head into squirting out of her hair follicles.

When I was sixteen, I came home with my hair cut short on one side only. At dinner, Dad was as always at the head of the table. I sat at his left keeping the short side of my hairstyle out of his view. I almost made it through the meal unscathed, until someone had to bring it up.

Dad freaked out. He threatened to kick me out of the house if I ever did something like that again. I was stunned. Compared to how other kids at school were misbehaving, I was a saint.

For weeks afterward, if we were out together and ran into anyone he knew, he'd ridicule my appearance and make jokes explaining my hairstyle – how I'd changed my mind halfway through; how I'd only had enough money to pay for half a haircut; how I couldn't make up my mind (foreshadowing the stereotype people would repeat to me later in life). It took me a long time to understand what my offence had been: nonconformism. Perhaps he saw eccentricity as a threat to our family's successful integration into Canadian culture. From that point of view, any deviance from the norm may have merited severe punishment. The only acceptable way for me to stand out from the crowd was by excelling. That was the lesson I learned, regardless what his intentions may have been.

The Hair Incident wasn't the first or last time Dad's extreme reactions would seem so out of proportion to my relatively innocuous infractions. That same year, when I was thirty seconds late to English class one too many times, he grounded me. Indefinitely.

That morning, Mr. Bedard marched me to the principal's office, who told me how disappointed my parents would be if he had to call them. But it sounded like he wouldn't call them if I shaped up immediately. So, I vowed to do so and went home, relieved. Mom confronted me upon arrival. I felt duped: the principal had called anyway. Dad would deal with me when he got home from work.

    I was upstairs in the study, a spare room we used for homework. My sister and I locked eyes across our desks when we heard the automatic garage door scrolling up. We tried to make out Mom and Dad's voices in the kitchen downstairs. The suspense was almost funny. I imagined the elastic grooves in Dad's form-fitting business socks polishing the hardwood floor as he came down the hallway. The boards creaked as he approached. He opened the door. No. He *threw* it open. The knob bounced off of the adjacent wall and the door slammed shut again. Then he walked in and with complete calm and composure said, "Don't bother asking me if you can do anything because the answer will be 'no' for as long as I feel like."

    I couldn't believe he was serious. Other kids were skipping classes, getting pregnant, smoking pot in the washrooms and dealing 'shrooms in the parking lot. And me? I don't think I ever lied to him, not even once. The doorknob left a circular impression in the wall.

    A few months after my forty-fourth birthday, I went in for a haircut. I was ready for a change. My stylist proposed a similar asymmetrical cut. "What the hell," I said. "It's only hair."

If we were making *ravioli*, the pasta sash would be laid over a mould. Ours was the size of an ice-cube tray. The bottom was enamelled in pale turquoise. Zig-zag serrations surrounded each square indentation in the stainless steel surface.

    Dad would lay the pasta along the bottom, then one of us would add the filling. Mom cooked pork and veal, then ground and combined it with seasonings and added a little egg and breadcrumbs for integrity. The bowl of meat was placed next to me. I would roll little balls of it and place one neatly into every pasta-lined square. Once filled, the edges of each square were moistened using a pastry brush. The layer of pasta Dad would drape over the tray was as smooth as an ironed shirt. He would use a rolling pin to press the pasta against the zig-zag serrations, sealing and dividing each square with a single motion. He peeled the extra bits of pasta away like extraneous cookie dough and pressed them back into the mound. Inverting the tray above a floured board or cookie sheet was the last step. Each identical pasta sack would be sprinkled with flour and separated so as not to stick to the others.

Mom ironed Dad's shirts in those days and he was always well dressed. For the office, he donned a tailored suit, silk tie and fashionable leather loafers. He also carried a *borsello*, a small bag of stiff leather with a handle at the top and a long strap for slinging it across the body. My uncles had the same sort of bag. Since I'd seen nothing else, I thought all grown men dressed this way for work.

Over time, Dad started leaving his *borsello* behind on the credenza. I asked him about it. His colleagues teased him about being gay whenever he carried it, so he stopped.

Ironically, though the *borsello* was a very common male accessory and a sign of refinement in 1970s Italy, these days discussion can be found on the Internet among Italian guys as to whether carrying the *borsello* is a sign of being gay. One advice-giver legitimizes the *borsello* by pointing out that Dolce & Gabbana as well as Armani featured it in their 2010 summer collections. Only in Italy would men make such arguments to reinforce their heterosexuality.

I can't help feeling somewhat disappointed in my dad for not holding fast in the face of Canadian prejudice. But I suppose eccentricity is the privilege of other Canadians, those for whom belonging is not in question.

Sometimes, the more you ty to fit in the more you stick out. Stampede Week was an excellent example. White-collar guys sat at their desks wearing cowboy clothes and tried the two-step after work while the real cowboys sweated and got dirt under their nails. During Stampede, Dad stashed his European style. He'd come down the stairs, bolo tie swinging over a freshly starched cowboy shirt fastened up to the last button. Worn for only ten days once a year, his Wranglers remained deep indigo for decades. They were ironed. The pant legs cut the same vertical crease as his pure-wool trousers. In the front entryway, he'd dust off his pristine cowboy boots. They were ankle-high. With a side zipper.

Thus duded up, he would stand in front of the mirrored closet door, as delighted as a kid. He'd check himself out, this way and that, herky jerky as C3PO, obviously thrilled with himself. The overall effect was as awkward as an eel modelling a lobster shell down the runway. But how could anyone bear to tell him?

I knew how it felt not to fit in. There was only one other Italian kid at our Catholic elementary school. Our grade five teacher was the only teacher in the whole school to be called "Ms." Everyone wore a different stylish outfit each day. Not me. My mom had been in Canada for ten years by then, yet she still dressed me in formal clothes for school as was proper in Italy. I had to wear the same wool skirt, leotards and collared shirt every day until they were dirty. Mom resisted my pleading for a daily change of clothes. "When you're a teenager and start to sweat," she said, "then you'll need to change every day." Any other child might have purposely dirtied her clothes, put a hole in her leotards with a staged fall on the tarmac during recess, or accidentally-on-purpose dribbled chocolate milk on her blouse. Not me. I was an obedient kid. I loved my family and adored my mom. I never wanted to disappoint or upset them. My family was my world. So I endured looking like a dork while the popular girls came to school in corduroys on Monday and painter pants on Tuesday, a pair of Adidas one day and Converse the next. Even their belts and socks changed colour daily.

I was different in so many more ways than fashion. Apart from writing my first story on a manual Olivetti at age ten, I was having sexual fantasies that would have shocked many adults. At age twelve, I invited my friends over with all their Barbie and Ken dolls. Once crowded into the bathroom, the same one in which Joan and I read *Hustler* magazines, I told my friends to strip their dolls and throw them in the tub together. At thirteen, I had full-blown crushes on female TV characters, especially Leather Tuscadero and Buddy. I was also crazy about a handful of boys at school. I kept a list ranked in order of intensity and updated it daily. At fourteen, I played a game called Teenagers. It consisted of receiving phone calls from imaginary boys and accepting dates until every day on the calendar was booked. Finally, when I was sixteen, some boys from class gave me a *Playboy* interview with my idol, David Bowie, in which he was asked how he'd met his wife. I'll never forget his reply: "We were both dating the same man." The classroom receded in my peripheral vision while the text seemed to magnify. I'd never been so focused on anything in my life. I read that section over and over again. I didn't understand why it was so utterly fascinating. It was the first time I'd ever been exposed to the concept of bisexuality.

In the eighteenth century, the *serinette* was invented to teach songbirds how to sing melodies. It was a small, hand-cranked mechanical organ resembling a pasta machine. My father's attempts to make me conform were just as absurd and futile as this ancient instrument. With each crank of the handle, he tried to make something uniform and predictable out of my diverse, adventurous nature. But his rigidity only entrenched my nascent eccentricity. Still, he did succeed in teaching me that my natural song was somehow wrong. I struggled to sing the proper tune for many years before I finally made sense of myself and found a way to live with integrity.

When making pasta, there are always casualties along the way. When a *tortellino* isn't perfect, when the pasta tears or filling squishes out the point, there is no fixing it. It simply *must* be eaten raw. Back then, we would feign horror and say, "Oh no! This one didn't turn out." We'd pop the bundle into our mouths, glinting a glance at our parents, who would feign disapproval and let us feel like we were getting away with something.

FINOCCHIO

I spent every Christmas with my family for forty years. It was the only time I saw most of them. Seeing all of them at once like that induced weeks of anticipatory anxiety. I'd feel the first tremors when the decorations went up in shop windows. By December twenty-third, the tremors would become quakes. A few hours before departure on the twenty-fourth, my anxiety would register on the Richter scale while I stood in front of my closet, preparing for the moment when I would walk through my father's front door and receive his inevitable judgement of my appearance. What could I wear to make it appear I wasn't chubby and poor? Was this tailored jacket too queer? Was that blouse too sexy? Would this outfit make my father treat me like his daughter? I went through variations of this for every family gathering, but Christmas was always the worst.

Sheldon, my living-in-sin boyfriend, supported me through it all. He never bemoaned our lack of Christmas traditions as a couple. We were both Grinches and our apartment never glittered with a single strand of tinsel.

At forty-one, I stopped celebrating Christmas with my family. You'd think it was because I'd finally had enough of all the angst. But no, my decision was prompted by something else. I had a girlfriend. And I was still with Sheldon. We were one happy and unusual family of our own.

This wasn't news to the adults in my family. I had come out to most of them a couple of years before meeting Tasha. My father and stepmother were the exception. His health was delicate, and in any case our connection was distant and tenuous at best. How would knowing that his daughter was a queerer version of queer improve matters? So this new triangular relationship of mine was not something that could be harmoniously integrated into our family traditions.

My siblings modified existing traditions to suit their evolving realities. Young children provided socially acceptable reasons for changes to dates, locations, mass times and menus. They had roomy houses to offer as alternate, more convenient locations for family get-togethers. In comparison to their homes, our apartment was a birdhouse and an impractical two-hour drive away. We were childless so perhaps it was assumed we'd accommodate others' needs. So no, the traditions didn't change to suit my evolution, and for twenty-odd years I did what worked for everyone else. Then I simply stopped.

That first Christmas I spent with my two loves provided useful insight into my family-related anxiety.

Tasha, Sheldon and I bought our first tree and put up decorations. I drove to Peppe's for *pandoro* and *torrone* and chestnuts. Tasha and I planned a menu and an open house for Boxing Day. I even felt a glimmer of holiday cheer and conceded to a few carols.

As the dreaded day approached, anxiety did not throw down its gauntlet. Instead, a miraculous calm reigned, and in that calm, a curious thing happened: I felt my mother's absence. How could I have celebrated twenty-five years of Christmases without feeling this, I wondered?

Emotion accreted in me like water becoming an icicle. Patiently, drip by drop, it metamorphosed into an imposing stalactite of frozen sadness, inexplicable and clinging precariously to the brink of my awareness. And when, incapable of bearing its own weight, my sadness lanced down from the eaves, it punctured the snowbank and disappeared, leaving my heart as smooth as glass. Upon that translucence, my lovers breathed their warmth, and a fragile tenderness bloomed in me like frost on a windowpane.

For the first time, I glimpsed my participation in family dramas for what it was. A smokescreen. Something to distract me from seeing that vacant place at the table, from feeling the resulting disjointedness of my relationships with most of those who still sat around it. That first Christmas was only the beginning. At each holiday meal with Tasha and Sheldon, I would comprehend another layer of loss related to family meals.

Unlike the imposing ebony surface of my past, the maple veneer of our simple table didn't need protection. Around a breathing bottle of Côte-du-Rhone, we scattered the autumn leaves Tasha and I had gathered on our afternoon hike. I placed glossy rosehips on each dinner plate, where they appeared to float like drops of blood on pools of milk. Four Japanese teacups matched the cobalt blue lines on the plates' rims. Each teacup bore a white circular seal, echoing the white-on-blue of the dishes. Suddenly, a memory of my mother's cobalt blue vase surfaced. There it was, poised on the ebony sideboard, its immaculate white interior at the ready, its gold leaf designs glowing in the sunlight from the bay window. I felt the grace and colour of these teacups resonate with that cherished object from my childhood, and wondered if I were glimpsing the reason for my loving these two colours together.

Our Thanksgiving menu featured a traditional dish from each of our childhoods. Sheldon would grill two links of Mennonite farmer's sausage, double-smoked fifty minutes away from his hometown. Tasha would prepare a classic Caribbean dish of peas and rice. I planned to braise a *finocchio* from Peppe's.

A *finocchio* is a vegetable called fennel in English. Imagine a white fist holding a bouquet of green fronds, fine as peacock feathers and drooping slightly at the top. The fist pries apart in crunchy layers of flesh whose flavour is reminiscent of licorice.

It's hard to find a *finocchio* with greens intact. Usually, the fronds are truncated about an inch above the bulb, leaving behind what looks like a fist with many thumbs all pointing in different directions. Or like a model of the human heart, complete with the stubs of amputated vessels.

Finocchio is also a derogatory term for a gay man. Imagine those drooping green fronds as a delicate hand flopping over at the wrist. I learned this word through my dad's use of it. Other times, when referring to homosexuals, he would flick his earlobe with a forefinger and say, "*orecchione*" – big ear. This word is not to be confused with *orecchiette*, a type of pasta that resembles a little ear.

That Thanksgiving, we invited the artist/nomad Caitriona. After Sheldon and I had transitioned to an open relationship, she'd been my first love. Once the pain of our break-up had subsided, my love for her morphed from eros into agape and we resumed a friendship. Now she's a member of our extended pod. I still think of her whenever I eat porridge.

When Caitriona arrives, Tasha exclaims, "Little Red Riding Hood!" She's wearing a reversible hooded cape, hand-stitched herself from plaid and bright red wool. She's leaner after her solitary, performance-art journey across the Canadian prairies. Riding an unshod horse, she often relied on water from sloughs, depended on gear tanned and stitched herself, played her hand-built instruments, and blogged about it all on her laptop.

I look around the table at our motley crew. A flower-patterned bandana holds back Tasha's afro-puff. Sheldon wears his usual

Wranglers and sweatshirt, this one with Dutch lettering on it that none of us understands and fear is derogatory. I've donned second-hand fleece running pants and a t-shirt bearing topo map contours. Compared to the high European style of family dinners past, we are very underdressed.

While the others chat, I think back to my walk with Tasha. I had to apologize for snapping at her. I'd been out of sorts all day. She wondered whether I was tired and frustrated with my writing progress. At this suggestion, a bolus of emotion rose. Forcing my voice past the constriction in my throat, I found myself complaining about the demands of my project, the isolation of writing, the emotional challenges of memoir. But the ache in my throat didn't dissipate, rather it tore down into my upper chest and was not relieved by crying. All the way home, I walked with this pebble in my emotional shoe.

And now, here I am, gathered with those I love most in the world, and I'm miserable. I'm irritated by minute details and judging everything. I try to throw in some stories and get cut off. Must I force my way into the conversation? I don't have the energy, so I give up and spend the meal subdued, nagged by the sense of having forgotten something.

Clearing the teacups and admiring their colour again, I remember something else about my mother's vase. She used to arrange her peonies in it. And then, for some reason, the final lines of Mary Oliver's poem, "Peonies," echoes in my ears: "to be wild and perfect for a moment, before they are/nothing, forever." I flee to the bathroom for another good cry.

Afterward, I discuss my strange mood with Sheldon. He says, "You get like that every time we have one of these pod dinners."

"It's because I'm disappointed," I tell him.

"I can tell," he says, "and I'm not sure why. The food was amazing. The company was fantastic."

Some recipes turn out so well they become the basis of all future comparison, the gustatory zenith to which all other food aspires. Such meals have a half-life. You must wait until the memory of their scrumptiousness decays before you can risk serving the same dish again. Tasha's brined turkey of the previous holiday was such a thing. That's why we didn't have it that day.

How long will it take, I wonder, for the memory of my childhood family feasts to decay? How long before my own humble meals cease to pale in comparison?

Pulling open the fruit drawer the next morning, I find the other thing I'd forgotten: the *finocchio*, still raw and waiting in its produce bag.

FEEDING

Walking in woollen socks within Birkenstocks of summer blue. Air at meditation temperature, perfect for focus: cool air in through nose, warm air out. Intuition guides me down the path instead of through the garden. And what a perfect diversion.

Tree fungus the size of a lunch plate. My fingertips slip from the rim to the stump that serves it up, bark draped like a towel over its arm. Atop the stump, a small pile of flakes, a squirrel's breakfast of dismembered cones.

A bass note vibrates in the ground. Strikes me still. Raindrops, I think, sliding randomly from leaves and needles to the forest floor. My upheld palms expect wetness.

Instead, I get spruce cones falling to the humus. Vaulting like gymnasts over branches, each cone rocks slightly upon landing to find its gravitational centre. Another cone impacts asphalt on the nearby road and bounces once before arcing back into place beneath the canopy. Unlucky others litter the road, soon to be flattened by tires.

Cones tap and rustle their way down through the boughs and free-fall the last few feet to lie on the ground, sticky with sap, awaiting the gentle acupuncture of tiny claw and tooth. Unconsumed, they feed roots and rhizomes instead.

I thought about how this white spruce was feeding the squirrels without intention. Cones are a matter of metabolic course, as is the September shed. The fruits of its summer labour, simply released. Squirrels fill their cheeks when the spruce offer up their bounty and not before.

This is how Tasha feeds those around her. Delicious dishes are the inevitable by-product of her being alive, as words are mine.

WEATHER

Today's weather: Fog with odd webs clearing. No breeze. Soon sun will angle through moisture and glint from filaments stretched across the trail.

A trail can be something you find snuffling like a bloodhound through the mist. Or it can be something left behind in crumbs of sound or scent. Others may track you, come upon you lurking lost in leaves or snow or moss. But they have to want to find you.

Letting go can be like walking in this weather: Fog with odd webs clearing. Braving the way most blurred by haze and spun with silk, we discover morsels of ourselves suspended in the filigree of memory. Our presence tears the web. And we stride free, trailing draglines.

MUSHROOMS AND MEMORY

"The fungi are in their own kingdom."
— Ben Gadd, *Handbook of the Canadian Rockies*

You mustn't imagine white, supermarket mushrooms. Instead, imagine moss-adorned mushrooms hugged by decaying leaves. Mushrooms whose caps know the shiatsu of rain and understand the responsibility of umbrellas. The kind that turn as black as squid ink and slide like oil against your tongue when sautéed.

Imagine wild mushrooms: puffballs, porcini and russula. Foraged personally. Eased by hand out of the soil from the very base of their stems so as not to tear away any identifying parts. Mushrooms birthed by earth and still dangling mycelial threads.

My mom loved foraging for mushrooms. She called it *andare a funghi.*

Andare a funghi means "to go mushrooming." I prefer the literal translation "to go to mushrooms." It evokes a pilgrimage, a quest for a grail, a whiff of the mountain going to Mohammad — whereas going mushrooming is merely an activity.

Mushrooms
cannot make their own food.
They take nutrients from the roots of green plants,
from dead
organic matter,
from feces
and soil.

In the same way, memory cannot create experience. Memory depends on human life, on the life of the human brain. It sustains itself on metabolites of perception — what we call "the past" — on the excreta of consciousness and the humus of layer upon layer of moments.

I don't remember much of my life before the age of ten. And since Mom died when I was sixteen, my connection to her depends on a mere six-year span of memory. And when I delve into that precious pond of images and impressions, I often encounter gaps. I remember how much she loved *going to mushrooms*. But what did she wear? How did she move? I only know there was a hat of some sort. And a basket.

My earliest memory of *going to mushrooms*: Dad putting mushrooms in the trunk of his baby blue Plymouth Belvedere and covering them with a Bolivian blanket before driving out of the parking lot.

Fines for mushrooming in a national park can go into the thousands of dollars. But I didn't know about fines back then. I only knew my dad was trying to get away with something. Mom hated this as much as I did. The feeling it gave me was familiar from airport Customs checks.

We'd come back from Italy once with suitcases full of expensive goods. He didn't declare most of it. A queen-sized camel hair blanket. A dozen or more shirts made of *filo di seta*, shiny silk thread. When I remember Dad in those days, he's always wearing one of these shirts in saffron yellow or navy blue. They were form-fitting with pointy, boned collars and a breast pocket over the heart into which he sometimes put his Polaroid aviators.

I don't recall any sweat stains on his silk shirt as he glided past Customs pushing that loaded luggage cart. Meanwhile, my scalp prickled and my belly felt full and empty at the same time. I gripped my mom's hand and avoided eye contact with big uniformed men, other travellers, cleaning staff – anyone, really. My fear was not as much of him getting caught as it was of being the one to give him away. I was incapable of telling a convincing lie.

I felt that same fear as we drove east and approached the national park gates with a trunk full of fungal contraband. But there was no checkpoint, no uniformed guard. After a few kilometres, Mom and I stopped checking behind us for red-and-blue flashing lights.

Was that clandestine foraging the genesis of my parents' mushroom plan? As my mom stooped to pick a choice edible that day, was my dad transfixed by her singular joy? Perhaps love led him to give his wife a gift: eighty acres of land where she could go to the mushrooms without fear of fines.

I like to imagine them waking up in bed together on a Sunday morning. Mom reaching out for her husband before her eyes even open and whispering, *"Andiamo a funghi."*

Mushroom
life is
mostly
invisible.
Memory is mostly hidden in the Unconscious.

To get to our property, we had to drive for a few hours. This meant we had to endure the surging and lagging sensations caused by Dad's inconsistent pressure on the gas pedal. It meant fumigating in a sealed chamber of Rothman's king-sized smoke. It wasn't as much a drive as a melty, stretchy, rewinding clock's worth of Dali-esque nausea and asphyxia.

Once we arrived, Dad would lift a loop of barbed wire over a wooden post to pull the fence open. He'd line the car tires up with

ruts in the ground and park just inside the fence. I would have my
door open before he even cut the engine, eager to dive into the
fresh air and silence. It was like snorkelling in tranquility.

Then, Dad popped the trunk. Accompanied by the ping of a
cooling engine, we slung little canvas *zainini* onto our backs. Mom
would don her denim bucket hat and take her square rattan basket
in hand.

We would leave the car behind, tall grass bent beneath the
chassis. The brush of the same grass against our jeans created a
static of peace, the soundtrack for the start of a beautiful day.

Sometimes, the neighbour's golden lab would run over to
greet us, barking. I'd pat his muzzle, careful to avoid the fleshy pink
bump on his head that grew larger by the visit as the tick gorged on
his blood.

We'd begin to scan the ground immediately, like pigs
hunting truffles. A network of footpaths and animal trails took us
into thick bush. Following our instincts toward the mushrooms,
we'd sometimes find ourselves foraging alone, out of sight of one
another.

I was never afraid of getting lost. I knew I could keep walking
until I hit fence, and follow that fence to another corner and then
another and eventually find the car. Besides, we'd blazed a trail
toward our meeting place. I just had to follow orange surveyor tape
or hatchet-marked tree trunks to reach the clearing we dubbed
Cathedral Square.

Cathedral Square wasn't just any old *piazza* with a crumbling
church. It was a square we'd cleared ourselves. In it, we stood on
humus, not masonry. We had branches instead of flying buttresses
and sky for a cupola. Our fire pit within a tripod of saplings inspired
more reverence than any altar, past or present.

The journey to Cathedral Square. Now *that* was the important part of the day. Without it, the square was only a picnic area and the fire just a grill for hotdogs.

I would wander in the trees, sensing everything. Solitary but not alone. Mom and Dad were out there somewhere. I could yodel out to them anytime. The silence flowed around me as intimately as warm water.

Once, in that stillness, Mom's voice reached me. The vibration of her sound resounded from wood and air and dappled light. It was an amalgam of song, yodel and exclamation. It was her joy-cry, set free as she found a rare choice edible at the foot of an evergreen.

In that moment, through her voice, my mom beamed herself to me; suddenly, she was *with* me. I didn't know exactly where she was. But I knew — more than ever before or since — I knew *that* she was.

This is my only memory of the sound of her voice. Sometimes, when I spot a mushroom's soft crown emerging from the earth, I can hear her calling out to me.

Why — out of all available samples of her speaking, yelling, and singing — why is this the sound bite that plays back?

A mushroom is only
the visible part of the mycelium,
an underground network of cellular
strands finer than human
hair.

A memory is only the sign of a buried neural net exchanging neurotransmitters in response to certain stimuli. A memory is the sign of metabolized life. Much more is stored than is ever exposed.

After the picnic lunch at Cathedral Square, the drive home. When my brother and sister were along, we would draw silly pictures of the mushrooms we'd found and made up fake Latin names. We gave *Lactarius deliciosus* an inverted cow's udder for a cap. The prized *Boleti*, which had pores under their caps instead of gills, became *Spongiformus yummiferus*.

At home, all the mushrooms would have to be laid out, spore prints taken, books consulted. Each fungus was vetted for edibility and safety. First, mushrooms with gills under their caps were separated from those with pores. The presence or absence of certain parts could tell delectation from poison. The annulus hitched around the upper stem like a little skirt. The volva sheathing the base like a little sock. This one bleeds white milk, that one bruises green, the other is riddled with insects. Puffballs were always the easiest. Once Mom and Dad were confident that we had a choice edible and not an *Russula emetica* or *Amanita felloides*, the mushrooms could be cleaned and the *risotto* process begun.

The kingdom of fungi cooperates with the plant kingdom.
As they feed on plant nutrients, fungi release enzymes,
thus producing essential elements for plants.
They release antibiotics, offering
protection from bacterial
infection. Fungi
loosen soil,
easing
movement
of
air,
of
water.
Memory feeds experience, transforming quotidien acts into
soul-sustaining moments. Memory strikes life like a bell, that we

may bathe in resonance. Memory inoculates us against oblivion. In the moment of recall, memory slackens our control, freeing the heart to join the blood in its visitation of every cell.

Risotto is to northern Italy as pasta is to the south. Rice itself is a defining feature of northern history and cuisine. Women from my parents' regions – Lombardia and Veneto – tended and harvested in the *risaie* of Piedmont and Lombardia during the nineteenth and early twentieth centuries. The *mondine* came from disadvantaged social classes. It wasn't work, it was exploitation. For meagre wages far from parity with the mens', they stood barefoot up to their knees in water, for extremely long hours of back-ruining labour. They wore wide-brimmed hats and kerchiefs over their faces for protection from the sun and teeming insects. These egregiously poor conditions led to an uprising in the early 1900s in which they fought for an eight-hour workday. *Se otto ore vi sembran poche* was their anthem: "If eight hours seem too few/you should try working too/and then you'll see the difference/between working and telling us what to do." The anonymously composed song warns, "We will do as Russians do./Those who do not work/will not eat."

Mom was from Milano. *Risotto alla milanese* is fragrant with saffron, rich with bone marrow and butter and cheese, spiked with white wine. She made her regional *risotto* often during my childhood, so often it's a wonder my chubby cells weren't saffron-tinted. *Risotto ai funghi*, however, was a special treat.

My parents were both good cooks and food was a high, daily priority. Often, Mom and Dad shared the kitchen, co-creating delicious meals. But they never taught me how to cook, per se. I learned by watching, by osmosis. I simply found myself dicing, mincing and seasoning in my own kitchen one day. My instinctual skills astonished me.

My mom belonged to that elite cadre of emancipated mother-chefs to whom recipes are like traffic signals to Italian drivers – merely suggestions. She added ingredients until it looked right, seasoned with a toss of the palm or a pinch of her finger, and baked things in a "hot" oven until it seemed done. She had a saying, "*Bianco di sale, nero di pepe.*" White with salt, black with pepper. Occasionally, she would pull an old recipe book from the shelf and remove the elastic band that held it together. She'd leaf through, tucking loose signatures back in as she went. Her finger would trace down the yellow page, pausing at the relevant detail for only a quick glance. Then she'd close the cloth covers, tap the whole book against the counter like a sheaf of papers, snap the elastic back in place and shelve it until she might have another question – oh, in say another six months or so. The dust-jacketed cookbooks and plastic boxes of recipe cards in the kitchens of my friends' homes were as strange to me as the milk they drank with supper, as foreign as the knick-knacks on their mantles.

Myself, I've never made *risotto* of any kind – and the kinds are many – but a packet of dried *porcini* from Peppe's has inspired me to make my first *risotto ai funghi.*

I know only this about making *risotto*: though simple, it takes time and patience. Liquid is to be added gradually, so that each grain attains a state of creamy goodness on the outside, while remaining *al dente* at heart. Like a woman who maintains her integrity while still revelling in love.

In preparation for making my own *risotto*, I've learned a few things. For instance, you need the right kind of rice. Only certain types of rice are capable of achieving risotto's quasi-divine amalgam of melting resilience. As a child, I never knew the word *arborio*. I had no notion of *carnaroli* or *vialone nano*. At our house, there was only ever one kind of rice: the right kind.

Mushrooms
are the mycelium's means of reproduction.
Mushrooms release spores.
Spores
grow
new
mycelia.
Memory spawns recollection spawns emotion spawns recollection.

One Thanksgiving Day, my stepmother served *funghi trifolati*, mushrooms sautéed in butter, garlic and parsley. It may well have been my last holiday meal at the old ebony table. All that wood and history dominate the dining room of her and Dad's row house in a senior's complex.

Only a subset of our family encircled the table that day, but I sensed other presences: the ghosts of our family conflicts and private lives — elephants so long ignored, they had sublimated into spectres. When we said *buon appetito*, I almost heard an echo down through the line of our ancestors.

Although that meal was a ghost of earlier holiday feasts, the magic of those times lingered like an aura. My niece unwittingly paid homage to one of my childhood games, sitting proud and princess-like in a purple velvet dress. The *funghi trifolati* moved me. I felt my stepmother was paying tribute to my mother, acknowledging her absence.

After eating, we went for a *passeggiata* along the paved paths of their complex. My niece held my hand. We came to a small rise in the path. She ran away from me. Then, stopping, turning, she ran toward me as though she hadn't seen me in years — face alight, arms flung wide. I squatted and threw open my own arms. She launched her little body into my embrace for a brief cuddle, then ran away again. She did this again and again.

Each time she ran off, her shiny black shoes mesmerized me. The way they reflected the late autumn glow. The way they tapped sound from the pavement like castanets. The way, propelled by her supple ankles, the shoes seemed to glide as carefree as a pair of skates.

Eventually, I realized the shoes were telling me something important: this was the first time I'd ever seen her run. Not for her the usual developmental milestones. Her cells preferred to simmer patiently until speech or movement became a pièce de résistance.

Over and over, at each collision, I echoed her joy. Each re-union was the first for her, celebrated as though after long absence.

We returned from that *passeggiata* under a spell. A rare harmony was modulating inside me. I hadn't felt this way with my family in years.

Six months later, a small gallstone would plug Dad's biliary duct, causing his pancreas to rupture and begin digesting itself along with other organs in his abdomen. Acute pancreatitis. He wouldn't be able to eat. Instead, a pale yellow paste would descend through a tube in his nose directly into his small intestine. I wondered whether he would ever eat again. Assuming he survived the illness. And that was a huge assumption.

The mycelium
produces a mushroom only when conditions are suitable.
Meanwhile, it carries on beneath the soil.
The mycelium can lie dormant or change shape,
exploring throughout the forest floor.
Some mycelial mats cover more than twenty-thousand acres.

I inherited a basket from my grandmother. The straw is woven into roughly the circumference of a pasta plate. It lacks the handle one expects of baskets. With lid on, the flattened ellipse reminds me of a mushroom cap or a flying saucer.

Tasha collects mountain plants — juniper berries, artemisia, wild sage — for use in poultices and natural skin-care products. Nonna's basket is ideal for foraging and small enough to lie horizontally in a backpack. So I gave it to her one morning before we set off on a late summer hike to a trio of translucent pools surrounded by pocked limestone cliffs, a moonscape painted with ochre pictographs and studded with climbing bolts and pitons.

Mushrooms lined the trail that day. Some were barely visible beneath a blanket of decayed leaves and spruce needles. I crooked a finger under a cap and felt pores, not gills, and that was good. "Most choice edibles do not have gills," I told Tasha. I waited until other hikers were out of view. Then, furtive as a thief, I used the long blade of my Swiss Army knife to gently pry the mushroom up from its base.

When you've lived in a national park as long as I have, removing anything from its wild place feels like commiting a crime even if it is outside the park boundary. I reassured myself, laying what I thought were *boleti* into the basket. As I covered them with a paper napkin, I saw a flash of the blanketed contraband in Dad's trunk.

I hadn't picked a mushroom since my childhood and I had no books on hand to aid in identification. We went online. *Lecceum* was our best guess, which is an edible, but I wasn't sure enough to eat them. The mushrooms sat on my bookshelf, shrivelling up in a paper napkin until I could bear to throw them away. For weeks, I felt slightly guilty about picking them.

A primary role
of fungi in the ecosystem
is decomposition.

It's about time I cooked my first *risotto ai funghi*. I weigh out the dried *porcini* from Peppe's. They remind me of some mushrooms I ate out of a baggie once, with Marcia.

My freckled friend had led me down a paved path meant for golf carts. Her manner was reminiscent of the jean-jacketed "heads" from my junior high days — gruff voice, lazy eyelids, atonal laugh. Her smooth, straight hair hugged her head. It fell from a rod-straight, gleaming centre part and curtained her ears and cheeks. Sunshine revealed her strands to be pure betacarotene.

Perfect turf extended in every direction. "Look!" I said, "It's the Emerald City. Squashed flat."

She had just given me the vilest-tasting mushroom of my life. A fibrous and bitter dried fungus out of a Ziploc. I had munched it like that, dry, straight from my cupped palm.

As we wandered across the green, the grass invited me down. Cross-legged, I rested my wrists on my knees with palms open to the sky. Clouds wafted into my lifelines. I hefted the weight of blue until mountain sky evaporated from my fingertips. In downward dog, prana shot out of my hands like silk from spinnerets, spinning down beneath the roots of bluegrass into some cosmic mycelium from which all life springs, through which all life is linked in chemical comprehension.

"Hey there."

Human speech seemed as distant as the Sea of Tranquility. I opened my eyes. Was that a white angular mushroom with round rubber stems, sprouting up beside me? I sat back on my heels and the fungus revealed itself to me. *Golfcarticus rubbiferous.* A golf cart. A guy inside a golf cart.

"Oh heyyyyy," I sighed. "I'm meditating. I'm doing the best yoga of my life."

Even though he was wearing sunglasses, I could see him squinting at me.

"Well, you can't do that here. You're in the middle of the driving range. You'll get hit in the head with a golf ball."

My friend and I climbed into the cart.

"How far away should we go?" I asked.

"Yeah, how far can golf balls fly?" Marcia asked.

I doubled over at the image of a glossy white sphere flapping its wings. Then the image vanished as I got lost in the sensation of my hair pulling back in the breeze. It felt as though each strand were rooted in the mycelium of the mushroom in my belly, threads now stretching as far as necessary to let me roam while staying connected.

He dropped us off on a hill behind the hotel. Marcie started to dance. I flew a kite until the wind died and we all floated down.

> When two mycelia meet:
> combat,
> deadlock
> or
> union.

The dried *porcini* rehydrate in lukewarm water while I chop scallion and measure out rice. I make stock with boiling water and organic bouillon paste. More boiling water simmers at the ready. Butter melts in the pan.

It smells great, right from the frying of the scallion and dry rice. Breathing through the nose is important. A characteristic scent wafts up like a smoke signal when the rice is perfectly toasted and ready for the wine. There it is, can you smell it? It's time to start adding the liquids. Chianti sizzles and evaporates. Next, the mushrooms along with the water from the soak, brown and fragrant. Add the stock and walk away for about ten minutes. Pluck a single grain from the pan with a fork tine. Chew carefully to judge its consistency. Add a splash more broth if the rice is too chewy. Wait for the rice to absorb it before testing again. Repeat. Meanwhile, grate *parmiggiano* (remembering of course, to leave some teeth marks in the block of cheese) and cut a piece of butter. When the rice has the right consistency, add butter and cheese and stir vigorously. Add minced parsley and cover.

I poured Tasha and Sheldon a glass of the Chianti. As I said *buon appetito*, none of us had any idea that, years later, we would leave the mountains to live in a mycophile's paradise.

The mycelium
links organisms together
beneath the surface.

BREAKING BREAD

My family ate dinner together religiously every day of the week. The kitchen table was always set by six o'clock because that was when my father got home from the office.

He'd come in from the garage with his camel-hair coat unbuttoned, lay his *borsello* on the credenza and stand his attaché case beside it. The pasta water would already be boiling – Dad insisted on pasta at least four times a week. He'd hang up his coat, slip off his loafers, and go into the bedroom to change. Shortly afterward, Mom would call out, *"Butto la pasta!"* and drop the dry pasta into the pot. This would be our time-check. We knew how long it took pasta to cook, and therefore, how long we had to wrap up whatever we were doing. We had to be sitting at the table precisely as Mom served the food or there would be hell to pay.

Mealtimes were sacrosanct. We answered the phone only to say, "We're eating right now. I'll call you back." Television was forbidden, as was reading at the table. My sister and I would always beg an exception for *Star Trek*, but it came on at six so our requests were futile. Even extracurricular activities were prohibited if they precluded being home for dinner.

During dinner, Mom had a "food first" policy. If you had something to say related to the food or the logistics of the meal, you could interrupt anyone. We started by appreciating the food, commenting on its flavour and texture or comparing it to the previous meal. Then we'd take turns talking about our days. My father and brother could be counted on to ignite the witty conversation. By the time we started our dessert of fruit and cheese, we'd be teasing and quipping and punning and washing it all down with hyperbole, irony and sarcasm, with a chaser of parody. Sometimes, Dad would tell us jokes in Italian. He never stinted on the ribald or profane content, which made my convent-raised Mom cringe. She would break her silence only to complain of being mocked — and perhaps we did have fun at her expense — but this led to the general opinion that she lacked a sense of humour. Now I wonder if what she actually lacked was the refined grasp of English required to seize our double-entendres and word play.

At some meals, Dad would open the English dictionary and we'd spend our last moments around the table cracking each other up by devising mock definitions and false etymologies, or creating portmanteaux from blending Italian, French and English words.

We would even debate for the fun of getting each other all riled up and playing devil's advocate. But occasionally, and more often as I got older, major arguments would erupt. I stared at my plate when tempers flared. Swallowing my food would require multiple sips of acqua Vichy. Sometimes, we reached a resolution during the fruit and cheese course. Other times, the anger and hurt endured long after the breadcrumbs were shaken from our tablecloth.

Whereas our mahogany kitchen table lay at the centre of family life, our dining-room table was a stage set only for special occasions. Its solid ebony surface, bare but for a tablerunner and centrepiece, stood encircled by empty chairs, waiting. The dining room's stillness evoked that of our church between masses. As a child, I was often drawn into that ambiance of peaceful expectancy.

I would stroke the wood, which was always smooth and warm. When the sun shone through the bay window, bright rays heated the ebony to a comforting, hot-water-bottle temperature.

Beneath my fingers, the subtle ridges of ebony grain felt like single strands of fine hair draped across a sheet. Together they mapped a miniature land of dry creekbeds and meandering oxbows, a magical wilderness that could expand every Christmas and Easter simply by adding a single leaf.

The legs of table and chairs alike spiralled down to the carpet like plump corkscrews. The chair cushions were gentle domes of velvet held to the wood by brass rivets. Those domes were so hopeful, so promising, like buns just beginning to rise. Only two of the chairs had arms, the ones at the head and foot of the table. I imagined these were thrones for the king and queen. On the dining room wall, a turbulent, dark-blue ocean crashed on the shore of an ornate gilt frame.

It was the perfect setting for re-enactments of *The Frog Prince*. In the sideboard, I even found props. Two pewter wine goblets and brass candlesticks. I'd don my "gown," a sheer peignoir set the colour of candied lilacs. Dressed in this relic of my mother's trous-seau, I'd sit on moss-green velvet and pass the afternoon eating invisible feasts and talking to frogs.

At other times, the tabletop was an altar and the goblet doubled as a chalice for reenactments of Holy Communion. Ours was an odd Eucharist. For hosts, my sister and I used bread slices. We tore or nibbled off the crusts, then squished the white mollica into thin discs and put them in the goblet. Then, completely unaware of committing sacrilege, we'd imitate the ritual as seen and practised in church.

My sister would pinch the host from the chalice with thumb and forefinger, hold it aloft and intone, "The Body of Christ," ar-ranging her face into a mask of holiness and looking up to the heav-ens (or in this case, to the white spackle ceiling). I would approach the "priest" with head bowed, right palm cupping left. Using the same controlled arc as an orchestra conductor, she would place the host into the "disciple's" palm. I would say "Amen," then eat the bread and make the Sign of the Cross. Whoever was the disciple had to impersonate the entire congregation. So, instead of going back to my pew, I went to the back of the imaginary line-up and re-cupped my palms. We took turns as priest and disciple, doling out and eating until we'd gone through an entire loaf of bread.

The same ebony tabletop was also used for holiday feasts. We would drape a padded cloth over the ebony tabletop to protect its surface, then dress it with a linen tablecloth, brass candlesticks, wine jugs of cut lead crystal, white plates with silver leaf borders, and silver cutlery.

And then came the food. Preparations began days ahead of time. We made the pasta by hand. We created the fillings from a combination of three different meats cooked three different ways, and hand-cranked them through the meat grinder while they were still warm.

Broths were simmered for hours, sauces concocted and seasoned to perfection, cheeses brought to correct temperature, prosciutto wrapped around *grissini*. When everything was ready – the *parmiggiano* grated, the wines decanted, the espresso ground, the grappa chilled, the mandarins and in-shell nuts jumbled artfully together in a bowl, the *panettone* and torrone displayed on the sideboard – we'd dress up. The women wisely wore skirts with elastic waistbands. The men would choose loose pants and belts of forgiving girth.

We'd sit down for *pranzo* around two in the afternoon. Each time a course was brought out, exclamations erupted. We'd inter-rupt our conversation to offer tasting notes to the chef.

Stomach space had to be budgeted, lest we be forced to pass on a favourite dish later. Seconds were always offered. Precarious things, those seconds. Should you have more lasagne and revel in a particularly velvety and balanced béchamel? Or save room for the roast pork, the artichokes, the *funghi trifolati*, or that extra slice of *panettone*? Then we'd get back to eating and drinking, non-stop storytelling and repartee. All the while, an eclectic mix of records spun on the turntable: Ramirez's *Misa Criolla*, Debussy's *La mer*, Xavier Cugat's *Viva Cugat!*.

Hours later, we'd wander from the table, painfully full. My brother, sister and I devised after-dinner rituals to cope with the over-indulgence. If eating *effervescenti* and lying on the kitchen floor didn't help, we'd hang upside-down from the back of the couch. Later, when my brother got a water bed, we would go there to lounge and groan together. We called it blorbing.

Meanwhile, my father would sit at the piano. He played by ear, and well. Sometimes he would sing along.

After my mother died, we had a single Christmas meal without her before my father married his old flame. Circumstances had intervened in their young love. After marrying other people and living completely separate lives in different countries, they had reunited in their mid-fifties and found the spark still alive between them.

My father did survive the pancreatitis.

After a talented (and noticeably butch) surgeon managed to save a nub of his pancreas. After almost dying a dozen times. After his wife spent over a year devotedly at his bedside, willing him to survive. Someone, perhaps the nurses, dubbed him Miracle Man. His kidneys barely functioned, he hardly remembered what he'd been through – the result of repeatedly being put into a quasi-coma with a drug euphemistically called Milk of Amnesia – but he was alive.

With him still in the hospital, I decided to go on meditation retreat anyway. During the last day of the retreat, I said to the ocean, "Dad, it's been a year. It's time for you to make a decision. Are you going to start eating again?" I got home several days later to uncanny news: he had taken his first solid food by mouth, likely around the time I had spoken to him in the ether.

How ironic. The curator of so many family feasts was the one who had endured a year of living without the flavour or texture of food. Those first bites must have taken great courage. By putting food in his stomach, he would have been facing the possibility that his remaining pancreas might re-erupt. Had he essentially decided that good Italian food was worth the risk? That living without eating wasn't worth it? From the moment of his first meal outside the hospital, sharing food with him became a new kind of feast.

That first Christmas after Dad's ordeal was my last with my family. He sat at the piano. With his niece by his side and his wife standing behind him, his fingers found the notes again. Drawing near, I made out the tune. "The Power of Love." As he began to half-sing, half-hum the lyrics, I met his wife's glistening eyes. She whispered something including the word "*miracolo.*" I thought about how their love had been rekindled after thirty years apart. I thought about how my niece had triumphed over genetic odds and survived several life-saving surgeries before age three to be humming along beside Dad, and how my sister's love for her had shown me the key to handling seemingly unmanageable things. And I thought about Sheldon, who loved me enough to let me be all of who I was, how he had held me through my panic attacks as I resolved my internalized biphobia, through the confusing euphoria of falling in love with a series of women. He had even held me when those women broke my heart. I thought of all this and had to agree: love is a kind of miracle.

How many grams of *lasagne*, *tortellini*, *risotto ai funghi*, *pasta alle vongole*, *pesto*, *salame* and *mortadella* does the average Italian male consume in the span of ten years? That's how much longer my dad would eat — and live.

No matter how much detail I cling to with my words, I will never re-create those childhood meals. The particular synergy of our family then — the alchemy of us, our wit and love and conflict, the wine and laughter and pleasure mingling with my innocence — that time is gone. Mom is gone, and her passage changed everything irrevocably.

Our childhood game was ironically accurate. Our table was indeed an altar, and our meals a form of communion. Like hosts, the food was meant to connect us to something beyond ourselves. Like Midnight Mass, our feast was a sensual ritual. My not cooking or eating Italian foods, my withdrawal from family celebrations — these were nothing less than a change of religion.

Writing these memories helped me to understand my bouts of binge-eating certain foods. During one particular yoga session, I greeted the usual ache in my throat but this time, it unfurled completely. The sensation began in my esophagus. I was able to breathe into it, to stay with it, until the ache inexplicably began to constrict even as it expanded. The pain was intense and strange, like the stretching apart of a partially healed wound. The wound lengthened to encompass my pharynx and widened until it claimed my lower jaw. Swallowing brought momentary relief, but the piercing, lacerating injury in my throat lurked in wait. It was then I understood. No matter how much soft, white bread, no matter how much melting chocolate, no matter how many sharp-edged potato chips I eat, I will never swallow the shards of grief lodged in my throat.

Uovo Sbattuto

My father was a teenager in Italy during the Second World War. His family of six lived on rations. All food had to be shared with his two brothers and sister.

He used to read the newspaper to his neighbour, an old professor who was nearly blind. When my dad finished high school, old Signor Piazza asked him what he wanted for his graduation present. And my father said, "*Un uovo sbattuto, tutto per me!*" A beaten egg, all to myself.

My mother didn't bake us cakes, cookies or pies. But she often made me *uovo sbattuto*.

To make this treat as she made it, you must first gingerly separate the egg. Crack the shell into equal halves. Ease the shells apart only slightly. Once you spy the yellow of the yolk, cup it in one half of the shell and let the egg white drip into a dish. Slide the yolk carefully into the other half-shell, letting more egg white drain.

Pass the yolk between one half-shell and the other until all the white has fallen away. You must keep the yolk intact during this process. If yolk mingles with white, it cannot do what's necessary for a successful dish.

At this point you may notice that the white clings to the yolk by a wrinkled white cord. Gently press the edge of the empty shell against the full shell until the bond is severed and all of the white has been separated. If too much white remains with the yolk, the dish will not turn out.

Drop the yolk into a bowl about the volume of a porcelain teacup. Repeat the process with another egg. The two yolks should slide against each other as though oiled.

At this point, Mom would cup the Pyrex bowl in the palm of one hand and take a fork in the other. She'd lean slightly against the counter, getting comfortable. Then she'd pierce the yolks with the tines and beat until the slippery egg yolk was transformed into a frothy cream and its pale yellow had faded into a delicate off-white.

She'd stir in white sugar and a spoonful of Marsala. After nestling strips of white bread on a plate beside the Pyrex dish, she'd place it all in front of me at the kitchen table, saying "*Solo d'inverno. E pesante.*" Only in wintertime. It's rich.

Warning: I've made Mom's *uovo sbattuto* sound easier than it is.

I tried to make it myself the other day. I separated the eggs perfectly. I duplicated the rhythm of her beating as though drumming along to a song playing in my head. The melody of fork against dish was just right, a duet of thud and click like the sound of a distant sprinkler. I beat and beat and beat, but the transformation didn't happen. Had I forgotten a step? My arms and shoulders cramped and gave out long before that *uovo* even hinted at being *sbattuto*.

When I told my sister about it, she said, "Use an electric mixer. It only takes a few seconds."

I don't recall my mother using an electric mixer on anything, ever. Besides, she whipped this dessert up by hand so easily, I hadn't thought a mixer necessary. I use a mixer to make it now, but it isn't the same.

When my friends finished high school, they asked their parents for Camaros. I tried to come up with a gift as simple and luxurious as my young dad's. There was no worthy equivalent. His daughter

had already savoured not one, but two beaten eggs all to herself –
complete with strips of fresh white bread! – and not once but many
times. Just because it was winter.

Now, whenever I'm on the verge of a big accomplishment, the
only gift I want is to hear my mother beating an egg for me in the
kitchen.

RECIPE

Tasha drops whole, unpeeled russet potatoes into boiling water. I clean the table with vinegar and water. Sheldon lifts the book he's reading to make way for my sponge. We're preparing to make my favourite Christmas dish for the first time: *gnocchi al burro e salvia*.

Gnocchi are a divinely simple amalgam of three ingredients: mashed potato, flour and egg. I prefer them drenched in melted, sage-infused butter.

I haven't had these in a long time. As if lactose and coffee intolerance were not enough for an Italian to bear, I now have gluten sensitivity as well. But thanks to Tasha's culinary talents, I will have homemade *gnocchi* again at last. She's worked out a rice flour and potato starch substitution.

Sheldon sits smiling, grey eyes dancing behind his glasses as he tracks our movements. I dust the end of the table with flour, remembering the large wooden board my parents once used. There are other ways to do things.

From still-steaming boiled potatoes, Tasha pulls skins with the asbestos fingertips of a chef. I press the naked potatoes through a ricer. No need to measure the flour: she adds it by eye, just enough to make it right. I slide an egg out of its shell onto the pile and she plunges into the ingredients, gathers and combines them with her hands into a mound and then begins to knead. I sprinkle more flour as needed until her fingers no longer stick to the dough.

Next, I cut away a piece of dough about the size of my hand. Sprinkling it with flour, I begin to press and roll gently against the table. Soon, the chunk has become a thick cylinder. Its warm, dry surface is smooth as skin to the touch. I suddenly feel the silky skin of Sheldon's biceps, resilient yet firm beneath my palms.

Once the cylinder is long and down to the thickness of a chubby finger, I cut it into pieces about the length of my thumb's first joint. When I brush them gently aside, the sound of dough sliding across the floured surface evokes that of naked skin against bedsheets.

I sprinkle a parmesan grater with flour. Gently, I take a joint of dough between thumb and third finger, and starting at the lower end of the grater, roll the dough up the surface with my index finger, pressing only hard enough to make an indentation, applying only enough pressure to pattern the dough with the grater's hexagons. I release my pressure at the top of the grater, letting the bundle roll freely back down onto the table. In this sound lies the distant echo of all the *gnocchi* made at my family's scarred mahogany table.

Each dumpling rests contentedly on the table like a miniature pot belly, complete with a small navel. As I repeat this process, I feel Tasha's belly beneath my fingers, her skin as fine as the texture of well-kneaded dough. I lift my finger from the indentation quickly, remembering how she dislikes me touching her navel.

Sage scent rises from the melting butter and the large pot of water is boiling. I hear hot liquid murmuring, waiting to receive the *gnocchi*, to transform them into something more resilient yet still yielding to the tongue.

The softness of the dough beneath my fingers, the laughter of my loves as they banter, pries apart the fist of my heart, and the layers of muscle unclench. In the spaces between I sense something riding my blood, something feral and sacred. My throat relaxes and expands into a shaft of light. A tendril unfurls, grows up into that light until it tickles and caresses the roof of my mouth like the delicate, playful fronds of a *finocchio*.

I toss one of the imperfect *gnocchi* into my mouth and embrace it with my watering tongue.

DECEMBER 7, 8:15 A.M.

The overnight Greyhound from Banff pulls into Pacific Central Station. I hobble down too-tall steps into frigid air. Uncharacteristically frigid for Vancouver yet reassuringly familiar to me, it would be recorded as the coldest day of the city's year. My first panic attack on BC soil is only hours away. Grief will grab its tail, becoming an Ouroboros with a circumference spanning years. Falling in another love is months away, the death of our family patriarch, years away. Myriad goals achieved and dreams come true and the breaking of my personal speed-of-sound-barrier await. My euphemism for this midlife relocation – the Vancouver Expansion – would soon prove to be literally true. But in this moment, I am a child again, exhaling clouds. Mom is zipping up my parka. She nudges my scarf down just enough to feed me a candy. I close my mouth around the sweetness and brave the cold.

SWALLOWING PENNIES

I follow the gleaming hardwood floor to the beam of light. Mom is pushing the sheers aside, exposing the bay window. The love seat warms its striped velvet like a cat in the morning sunshine. My toes are warming up, too, there beneath the hem of my cotton nightgown.

"Mom, I swallowed a penny."

She rushes me to the hospital. They pump my stomach but find nothing. I'm confused.

"*Bugiarda!*" my mom calls me. Liar.

"But I swallowed it. I did."

"*Quando?*"

"Last night."

"Before you went to bed?"

"After. While I was asleep."

"You were asleep. How could you swallow a penny while you were asleep?"

"I always do things while I'm asleep."

"*Tonta! Sognavi.*" Silly girl, you were dreaming. She explains how dreams are not real. What happens when you're dreaming and what happens when you're awake are two separate things. Never confuse the two.

This is the moment. The one where my orbit of seamless existence decays and life fragments into two distinct states of being. Awake. Asleep. The moment of my exile from the womb of waking dreams, in which life is an infinite blossom of moments unfurling one into the next, be it night or day.

I'm not retrieving this event from memory of the experience.

In absence of actual recollection, I must conclude that my knowledge of events is second-hand.

If memoir is the process of making stories out of memories by recreating them in our imaginations, what do you call it when you write a memoir of someone else's recollection, a memoir *they* told *you*?

I have so many questions.

Did the stomach pumping actually occur? Wouldn't the attending physician have x-rayed me first, to determine where the coin was lodged before pumping?

Did the pumping happen in my imagination at the mere suggestion of the procedure? Did I confound that imagination with actual experience, just as I had blurred the line between dream and wakefulness?

Perhaps I did indeed swallow the penny and I simply do not recall it. Somewhere in my body, would I find a residue of my indignation at being falsely accused of lying?

I was not lying. I'm certain of that. If I had been, how could I have submitted to the unpleasantness of stomach pumping? As I saw the hose making for my open mouth, wouldn't I have recanted? No, I wasn't lying because to me, my dream was real.

So many questions without answers, so many memoirs of memoirs unwritten, all lost when my mother died, leaving anecdotes untold. If with her last exhalation she could have released all her knowledge and experience, murmured everything left unsaid, I would have inhaled that final blessed wisp of her essence like the last molecule of available oxygen from a deep-sea diver's tank.

My dreams flicker into consciousness like the glimmer of a trout leaping for a fly and disappearing back into the lake. Or they stand before me as definite as a moose raising his grass-draped muzzle from beneath a marsh, as marvellous as the sparkling water cascading from his antlers in the sunlight. Sometimes they form an inky beast, oozing slime and absorbing any trace of illumination. Often, they are cinematographic and project onto an invisible screen, like 3-D holographic blockbusters.

I awake believing every scene, but eventually I look for the penny. I feel across the rumpled surface for Sheldon and tell myself, "Feel that bellows in his ribs? He's alive." Or I ask Tasha, "Are we on a cruise ship? Did you just leave me for a tall black man?"

Memoir arises in the chasm between a memory and its source experience. Writing memoir irrevocably alters its subject matter. What feels like a reclamation is only another permutation of the incessant storytelling that forms our reality. From memories as impressionistic as dreams we weave our narrative web and become ensnared.

Brain researchers now know that memory is not static, that memories can be biochemically erased as they are being formed, and erased as they are being recalled. The implication – that recollection is in fact re-creation – reveals memory as an imaginative act. And the more you revisit a specific event, the less accurate it becomes. The truest memory is the unrecollected one.

Writing is the pump by which memory's contents are suctioned into the light of scrutiny. From then on, memoir is fabrication.

If unconscious memories are the only authentic residue of my existence, then my only true life is an unremembered dream.